Contents

Published by
Scots Independent (Newspaper) Ltd
51 Cowane Street
Stirling
FK8 1JW
Scotland
www.scotsindependent.org

ISBN: 978-0-9572285-0-4

Printed by Peters Design & Print
Tel. (01888) 563589

Foreword

Between January 2006 and December 2011 Ian Goldie wrote month by month on aspects of our ongoing campaign for independence. From him we accepted food for thought and some deeper grasp of issues and arguments. But even articles and columns which impress tend to lose their impact as time passes. We remember having read that, somewhere , sometime. But where? and when?

What an eye-opening experience it was for his colleagues at the Scots Independent when they read at one sitting as it were the full range of what their old, lost friend had written. We quite suddenly realised that he had left us as effective and coherent an analysis of all issues affecting independence as exists, or is likely to be compiled now. Thanks to him between now and Referendum Day our movement has available to it a statement of principles defined and arguments deployed which will greatly benefit all who must speak up for independence.

Ian Goldie comes across as a careful, calm and courteous observer and recorder. His language is clear, simple and straightforward. His case is logical and well-informed and his many telling insights reveal his sensitive understanding of responsible politics. We see our purposes served and enhanced by Ian's work and we are urgently anxious to spread his influence as widely as we can.

Most moving for me is his last article "Winning the Referendum". The arguments are there of course, but even more to be valued and honoured, and so typical of him, is his plea which he calls "The Need for Courtesy, Decency and Moderation." Good politics, yes, but good principles too from a fine man.

James Halliday

CHAPTER 1

The leopard does not change its spots

Labour now want to change their system because it does not favour them as much as it should.

When the Scottish Parliament was set up, it was recognised that the old first-past-the-post system of electing representatives was discredited and could not reflect a modern complex democracy.

So the Lib Dems and Labour agreed on a kind of proportional system - the old first-past-the-post system of 73 individual seats, and a top-up list system for 56 Members of the Scottish Parliament (MSPs) to balance to a certain extent the bias in the old system.

This gave more proportionality, but had the disadvantage of creating two types of MP - a single member elected by a single constituency, and list members elected by a group of eight constituencies, with seven list MSPs per group of constituencies.

Because of the historic strength of the Labour party, Labour ended up with a disproportionate number of the single member constituency MSPs. The other parties were to a great extent represented by list MSPs.

To its discredit, the Labour party, who set the system up, has constantly tried to undermine its own system, principally by denigrating list MSPs as second-class MSPs or failed politicians or back-door MSPs.

Some time ago they began to suggest that they wanted to change the present system, a change that would be of terrific benefit to Labour and undermine all the other parties. The latest proponent of change is Scotland Office minister David Cairns.

The idea is that candidates should be barred from standing in both the constituency and the party list at the same time. Well, of course, this is great for Labour, as they know where their safe seats are and many Labour candidates will be assured of being elected.

But it is certainly not so good for the other parties.

Let us say you have a first-class SNP candidate in the Glasgow area. He or she will normally be selected to fight a constituency, but will have little chance of winning, losing probably to a Labour Mike Watson equivalent or worse. Then that excellent candidate would not be allowed to stand for a list seat, even although they might have come top of the list!

This system, if adopted, would be a great political fix for the Labour party, and deplete the quality choice for all the other parties.

It probably will not happen, but it just shows you how far the Labour party might go to undermine democratic choice in its own interests; the leopard does not change its spots.

The day will come, of course, when the trends of recent years will lead to the Labour party being far less powerful in Scotland than it is at present. So in the longer term this is not even a good idea for future Labour candidates.

SI 923 January 2006

CHAPTER 2

Oil revisited with Lord Healey

We could have been another Norway – the richest country in Europe – if not the world.

Well, what a to-do following the BBC Radio 4 programme on how Westminster in the 1970s swindled the Scots out of billions of pounds worth of oil revenues.

The lying, the deceptions, the misinformation, the undermining of Scotland - all was revealed.

The whole episode is a disgrace, of course, but what I found really revealing were some of the comments from Dennis Healey, Labour chancellor at the time.

Lord Healey, as he now is, was so pleased that the Labour party had had such stalwarts as John Smith, Donald Dewar and Helen Liddell around at the time, for they were able to keep the rest of the party in Scotland on side - i.e. the London side.

Healey also suggested that these politicians recognised that their own careers would be much more important as representatives of Great Britain than they could possibly be as representatives of tiny Scotland.

The cost, of course, was the sell-out of the oil to London.

So for the personal ambitions of a few Labour politicians, Scotland lost the oil and with it the chance to transform our nation. We could have been another Norway, now the richest country in Europe, if not the world, which has used part its oil revenues to create a new transport infrastructure and an oil fund for future generations.

Our oil was squandered in the 1970s by an incompetent Labour government determined to use the bonanza to get it out of its economic black hole, squandered in the 1980s by the Conservatives on unemployment benefit for the unemployed created by Mrs Thatcher's policies, and squandered since 1997 by Labour's vainglorious foreign interventions and wars under Tony Blair.

When challenged about all the disinformation that had gone on, Healey's comment was: It was possible for intelligent Scots to work it all out for themselves and not depend on the British Civil Service.

What cynicism! What hypocrisy!

Many intelligent Scots had worked it out for themselves, but they were a small voice when ranged against government propaganda and the so-called Scottish media, especially the likes of the Daily Record. How could ordinary Scots find things out for themselves when our highest-selling newspaper was regurgitating government propaganda?

SI 925 March 2006 also Special SI May 2006

CHAPTER 3

Failed states index

I was on holiday in Portugal recently and picked up a copy of The Portugal News – Portugal's National Newspaper in English.

What caught my eye was a headline on the front page: Portugal Stands Strong, with the following commentary: Independent Study depicts Portugal as one of the most successful and solid states in the world. This was based on something called the Failed States Index.

I had never heard of the Failed States Index before, but the study was published in the American magazine Foreign Policy and was conducted in conjunction with the Washington-based Fund for Peace. Who they?

Anyway, it is in its second year, and is interesting chiefly for two reasons: the order it places states in (especially those they consider to be the most successful) and its methodology.

Top rated states for stability and lack of vulnerability are:

1 Norway	6 New Zealand	11 Austria
2 Sweden	7 Australia	12 Japan
3 Finland	8 Canada	13 Netherlands
4 Ireland	9 Belgium	14 Singapore
5 Switzerland	10 Denmark	15 Chile

No surprise in the top six, then, which have all the great ingredients for success – small, democratic, politically advanced and independent.

I was slightly surprised that Belgium came so high, and very surprised that Chile came in at number fifteen. (But then, I can't claim to be knowledgeable about Chile.)

Portugal, by the way, came seventeenth, immediately ahead of the UK, France, the USA and Italy.

The methodology is interesting. There are twelve indicators, and each country is given a score for each indicator out of ten. These are then totalled. The higher the state scores, the less stable it is. The indicators are divided into

Social Indicators (1-4), Economic Indicators (5-6), and Political Indicators (7-12). They are:

Mounting Demographic Pressures
Massive Movement of Refugees or Internally Displaced Persons
Legacy of Vengeance–Seeking Group Grievance or Group Paranoia
Chronic and Sustained Human Flight

Uneven Economic Development along Group Lines
Sharp and/or Severe economic Decline

Criminalization or Delegitimization of the State
Progressive Deterioration of Public Services
Suspension or Arbitrary Application of the Rule of Law or Widespread Violation of Human Rights
Security Apparatus Operates as "State within a State"
Rise of Factionalized Elites
Intervention of Other States or External Actors

Search for the site under Failed States Index or go to:
http://www.fundforpeace.org/programs/fsi/fsindex.php

SI 929 July 2006

CHAPTER 4

Independence - natural and normal

Last month I promised that over the next ten months I would devote one article in each of my monthly sessions to arguments in favour of independence.

Bear with me if you feel you've heard it all before – lots of folk have not!

Two of the most compelling arguments for independence are as follows. History seems to be on the side of independence movements. And the independence of nations is both natural and normal.

Does anyone doubt that the Scots think of themselves as a nation?

Throughout history, many – especially smaller - nations have been forcibly united with or dominated by larger nations. But almost always, the smaller nations have ended up by struggling for and eventually winning their freedom.

For the past eight hundred years or so this struggle has been going on.

Remember Switzerland's William Tell fighting off the domination of Austria in the 1290s?

Scotland about the same time was fighting off English domination under Edwards I and II.

In the late sixteenth century the Dutch won their freedom from Spain.

And in 1640 Portugal too won the fight against Spanish rule.

Two hundred and thirty years ago we saw the United States win its freedom from the British – one of history's greatest triumphs for freedom, and one that all independence movements can still learn from. Within fifty years Spain and Portugal's South American colonies too had gained their independence.

In the last hundred years we have seen freedom being won in Europe (not to mention the rest of the world) by the following, among many others:

Norway (1905, from Sweden)
Finland (1917, from Russia)
Estonia (1918, from Russia)
Latvia (1918, from Russia)
Lithuania (1918, from Russia)
Hungary (1918, from Austria)

Poland (1918, from Austria/Germany/Russia)
Ireland (1922, from Britain)
Iceland (1944, from Denmark)
Estonia (1990, from USSR)
Latvia (1990, from USSR)
Lithuania (1990, from USSR)
Croatia (1991, from Yugoslavia)
Moldova (1991, from USSR)
Slovenia (1991, from Yugoslavia)
Slovakia (1993, from the Czech Republic)
Montenegro (2006, from Serbia)

None of these countries is remotely interested in retreating under the wing of their former rulers.

Some of them, especially in Northern Europe, have been outstandingly successful. Others have not yet had the time to prove themselves. But I am quite sure that, with self-government and democratic systems, they will make progress they have never known before.

Does anyone really think now that, for instance, Holland or Norway or Ireland would ever have been the successes they are under Spanish, Swedish or British rule?

Does anyone really think that the former USSR Baltic states would have been better off under the old system?

Personally. I am as certain as I can be, that unless Scotland gains its independence, then within fifty years the Baltic nations, so far behind us today, will have left us standing.

The development of European history has shown that the old argument for colonialisation – "Aren't we all getting together in the modern world?" - is unsustainable. The old empires – Portuguese, Spanish, Ottoman, French, British, Austrian, Communist – are almost all dead and gone.

Yes, we'll get together with other countries, *if we want to*, as equal members in a looser and confederal union, but not as part of a union imposed against our will.

SI 931 September 2006 also Special SI November 2006

CHAPTER 5

Simon Heffer, Basher of the Scots

Scotland : "a distant province or satellite state."

At the end of November, Simon Heffer, a journalist with the London Daily Telegraph, wrote an article inspired – if that is the word – by the Labour Party's Scottish Conference – the one where Gordon Brown and Douglas Alexander forsook Westminster to come north to bash the Scottish National Party.

I missed the article, but its final paragraph was emailed to me by my nephew. It reads as follows:

"I know this is horrid for Gordon Brown, who like Napoleon, or Stalin or Hitler, aspires to come from a distant province or satellite state and take over the mother country. But he and his friends started this process; it is a shame given how very brilliant we are always being told he is, that he wasn't clever enough to realise how we might finish what he started."

Now this is fascinating.

Firstly, while politically I am opposed to Gordon Brown, I feel the juxtaposition of his name with those of Napoleon, Stalin and Hitler, is both ludicrous and sinister. It is simply smear by association. Had these words appeared in any Scottish newspaper there would have been expressions of outrage from letter writers and other media.

Secondly, the view of the Scottish nation as "a distant province or satellite state" says it all about the attitudes of many active in the media in London.

Thirdly, the view of England as the "mother country" reinforces the idea that other countries in the so-called United Kingdom are simply there to follow what the "mother country" dictates.

It is all very reminiscent of the late Enoch Powell who, when talking of the "English kingship" said :

"English it is, for all the leeks and thistles and shamrocks, the Stuarts and Hanoverians, for all the titles grafted on it here and elsewhere, "her other realms and territories", headships of Commonwealth and whatnot. The stock that received all these grafts is English, the sap that rises through it to the extremities rises from roots in English earth, the earth of England's history."

To return to Heffer's article, it is curious how, for him, all the constitutional ills of the Westminster Parliament are transposed from politicians in general, to Labour politicians in particular , to Scottish Labour politicians and finally to the Scottish electorate.

It seems to be all the fault of the Scots that Scottish Labour politicians are successful in their own small Westminster sphere, that England does not have its own parliament, that Scots are "subsidised" by the English.

Mr Heffer never seems to ask himself why English Labour politicians must be of such poor quality that the Scots take so many top positions, why England never campaigned for its own parliament until now, and why- if we believe his figures- Scotland is doing so poorly run from Westminster that it has to be grossly subsidised.

But he does go on and on. Really, how long can this old Union last when such influential English commentators hold the Scots in such obvious contempt?

SI 936 February 2007

CHAPTER 6

Scotland too wee to be independent?

Living standards based on seven key tables.

Here is an interesting quote from Lord Forsyth of Drumlean speaking on 25 January this year at the House of Lords debate on the Union between England and Scotland:

"An independent Scotland would struggle to catch the waiter's eye in Brussels. It would be a country of 5 million in a community of half a billion."

This is the same Lord Forsyth who, as plain Mr Michael Forsyth, was Conservative Secretary of State for Scotland, and responsible for the Tory demise in the 1997 general election in Scotland.

His is a statement that reeks of arrogance and of contempt - contempt, not just for Scotland, but also for all our other small nations.

For Lord Forsyth, such countries cut a pathetic figure, have no voice, and seem to skulk in some downtown Brussels joint, trying to order a crumb – without success.

So my Lord Forsyth indulges in dire predictions. Let us take a look at the established facts.

Just how are these small pathetic countries of northern Europe doing, and doing relative to Britain?

Let us take a look at living standards based on seven key tables in the 14 countries of northern Europe. Six, Like Scotland, have a population under 5.5 million: Iceland, Luxembourg, Ireland, Norway, Finland, Denmark. There are three others under 9 million: Switzerland, Austria, Sweden.

First, let's take **GDP per person.** Here are the latest ratings taken from the 2007 edition of the Economist's "Pocket World in Figures".

1 Luxembourg 2 Norway 3 Switzerland 4 Ireland 5 Denmark
6 Iceland 7 Sweden 8 Austria 9 United Kingdom
10 Finland 11 Netherlands 12 Belgium
13 France 14 Germany

Now, of course, GDP is a good rough measurement of a country's economic performance, but it does not claim to be everything.

So how about the **Quality of Life Index?** Here are the results.

1 Norway 2 Iceland 4= Luxembourg and Sweden 6 Switzerland

7 Ireland 8 Belgium 9 Netherlands 10 =Denmark and Finland
12 UK 13 France 14 Austria

More generally, how about the **Gender-related Development Index?** This shows how well women do relative to men, with the most advanced countries generally coming out near the top.

1 Norway 2 Iceland 3 Sweden 4 Switzerland 5 Luxembourg
6 Belgium 7 Finland 8= Ireland and the Netherlands
10 Denmark 11 UK 12 France 13 Austria and Germany

And what about **Global Competitiveness?** Here are the northern European figures.

1 Iceland 2 Denmark 3 Switzerland 4 Luxembourg 5 Finland
6 Ireland 7 Norway 8 Austria 9 Sweden 10 Netherlands
11 UK 12 Germany 13 Belgium 14 France

Or then again, how about general health? Just take a look at the latest **Life Expectancy figures.**

1 Iceland 2 Switzerland 3 Sweden 4 Norway 5 France
6 Austria 7 Belgium 8 Finland 9 Germany 10 Luxembourg
11 Netherlands 12 UK 13 Ireland 14 Denmark

And how do we all do on the **Lowest Infant Mortality** scale?

1 Iceland 2 Sweden 3 Norway 4 Finland 5 Belgium
6 France, Germany and Switzerland 9 = Austria and Netherlands
11 Denmark 12= Luxembourg and UK 14 Ireland

Finally, let's take a look at **Income Equality** – how a nation's wealth is spread throughout its population. (These figures are taken from the UN/CIA Income Inequality Indices. I have found are no figures for Luxembourg or Iceland, so this last table covers only 12 countries. Latest year figures.)

1 Denmark 2 Sweden 3 Norway 4 Finland 5 Germany
6 Netherlands 7 Austria 8 France 9 Belgium 10 Switzerland
11 Ireland 12 UK

Summary

In these seven important areas, out of the fourteen north European countries, Britain languishes in the bottom four places in six of them. Her highest position is 9th – still in the bottom half.

So when you hear folk talk of the Union dividend, now you know from official figures – there is none!

SI Special Spring 2007

CHAPTER 7

Scotland – the invisible country

In previous articles I have tried to concentrate on the positive arguments: (a) Independence is natural and normal (b) Independence is psychologically good for countries and people and (c) Independence will restore democratic government to Scotland.

I would now like to reflect on some of the things that Scotland suffers from as a dependent nation and on the transformation that independence would bring.

Firstly we would not be run by a parliament with over 80% of English members, many of whom have little knowledge of Scotland. Constitutionally, we would have our own parliament, putting Scotland's interests first, having the time to solve, and being able to concentrate on solving, problems particular to Scotland. In a minor way, this has already been started by the presently devolved parliament.

Secondly, the present first-past-the-post system, leading to "elective dictatorship", would be consigned to history. With a good system of Single Transferable Vote, we would have a balanced parliament that would reflect the will of the Scottish voters.

Thirdly, from an international perspective, Scotland would no longer be an "invisible" country. We would double our number of MEPs in the European Parliament (if Scots choose to remain in it) and have Scottish men and women- as of right- taking part with their colleagues from the other countries in its various institutions.

We would also have our own seat in the United Nations, as other countries do.

Fourthly, we would not have a foreign and defence policy based on the desires or delusions of the Westminster government. Our own Scottish government would choose whether or not to be a part of NATO, and we would almost certainly opt not to have Trident or any other weapons of mass destruction based in our waters or on our land.

We would have our own foreign policy and have contacts with other nations in the same way as other small European countries have.

Fifth, we would not build an over-capacity of power stations, and there would be no danger of Scotland becoming a dumping ground for other countries' nuclear waste.

Sixth, nor would we, without the agreement of our own government, have weapons ranges that would pollute our shores. Low flying planes would be subject to much tighter restrictions.

Seventh, our present policies on oil and fishing would have to be totally reviewed.

Eighth, we would not be subject to a barrage of news filtered through a BBC London perspective. News would be from a truly Scottish perspective – just think of the news of the Iraq war from a Scottish viewpoint, rather than from a Brown/Blair perspective.

These, then are just a few of the changes an independent Scotland would see. They stem from the basic fact of independence, and would happen irrespective of party.

SI 937 March 2007 *First published in The Flag in the Wind.*

CHAPTER 8

The anti-independence case.

If you have ever tried to get Unionist politicians to outline their arguments for the Union between Scotland and England you have probably found a great reluctance to come up with the goods, so that is why I welcome the attempt by Scottish LibDem president and MP Malcolm Bruce to explain his point of view in *The Herald* last month.

Here are some of his points:

1 The stage on which Scots could perform would shrink dramatically.

2 We would lose the influence the UK has as a big player in the EU and the UN.

3. We would have to construct our own welfare state and external relations.

4. We would no longer influence England's direction of travel.

5. Conservative England may quit the EU, 'leaving them free to discriminate against the Scots'.

6. We need a modern Union that 'offers a partnership fit for this century and defeats small-minded separatism wherever it is coming from'.

Referring to the points above:

1. Not so. When we become independent, actual Scots will represent the interests of Scotland in Europe and the United Nations. In the EU, Scotland as Scotland will not be excluded from the Council of Ministers, and we will more than double our representation of MEPs. We will appear as Scotland in the Olympic Games and have many more competitors taking part. Scotland simply just does not exist in these areas. We are an invisible country.

2. Scotland as Scotland has **no** influence in the EU nor the UN. Scotland is a mere adjunct to English policy. Worse, our assets can be traded off without reference to the wishes of the Scottish people, as our fish was in the 1970s.

3. Other small countries have shown that they are far better at constructing their own welfare state than Britain. And our external relations would

be built on the basis of being one nation in the international community. We would not approach other countries with the arrogance so typical of Westminster politicians.

4. Does Scotland have any influence at all on England's 'direction of travel'? Basically, that is up to England, and we should not interfere.

5. It is possible, but highly unlikely, that England would leave the EU. However, it seems a strange argument that we should stick with England because they are so nasty that they would turn against us if we went our own way.

6. This is a real give-away. Mr Bruce cannot bring himself to use the word independence. To win his argument he has to turn independence into 'small-minded separatism'; I wonder if he has ever visited the Irish Republic, Iceland, Norway, Finland and other states that have won independence to castigate them for their 'small-minded separatism'

It seems to me that there is one basic difference between those who argue for independence and those who argue against. Those who are in favour of the Union have a 'great state' mentality. For them, big is better, and you must belong to a state that is really important in this world. Small countries to them seem almost irrelevant.

Hence Mr Bruce's talk of 'influence', 'big player', and his apparent belief that smaller countries have no part to play in world affairs.

Those of us who believe in independence accept that Scotland is a small country, but we want to be a good neighbour, friend and example to others. Incidentally, we also want the highest possible standard of living for our people, which is something the small countries of northern Europe have achieved in spades, unlike their large neighbours.

SI 942 August 2007

Adapted from the Flag in the Wind

CHAPTER 9

The case for Independence

The English think that Scots have too big a say in running Britain

Time and time again we hear that Scotland cannot exist as a country on its own. Very seldom are convincing arguments advanced for this view – mere assertion appears to be deemed enough.

But sometimes there are straws in the wind and I have tried to glean some of the thinking behind the Unionist assertions.

Scotland is too small to prosper

Fortunately, we now know that other small independent European countries are doing far better than we are, especially Norway, with its control over its own resources such as oil and fish. It is a fact the small countries of Western Europe are in the lead in almost any table of prosperity or quality of life you care to consider. Why should Scotland be any different? Are we just inferior?

There's nothing here

This is the typical cry of the uneducated. For its small population, Scotland has plenty of rain (very important), lots of oil (important, but not vital), lots of fish in its waters, a huge coastline, lots of land for farming and recreation, great potential for renewable energy, a good ratio of population to area, a modern and very important financial sector, a relatively highly educated population, a stable and relatively modern democratic system, an advanced media system and has a history of relatively liberal and enlightened attitudes.

Quite apart from that, throughout the country there are literally thousands of activities and businesses large and small that all contribute to our national life.

Scotland could not exist without English subsidies

If this is indeed the case then it is a scandal that the present Unionist system has so impoverished our country that we cannot stand on our own two feet like other small countries. With all the resources that Scotland has, what a condemnation of the present system!

I do not believe, however, that the situation is as bad as that, but there can be little doubt that Scotland has been sadly held back by the present system.

We just don't have the talent to run our own country

Because of the historic emphasis placed on education here, Scotland has a tradition of excellence in many spheres. Indeed, a recurring complaint among English people is that the Scots have far too big a say in running Britain. We have churned out great scholars, thinkers, engineers, doctors, businessmen, architects, explorers, sailors, soldiers and candlestick-makers – not to mention statesmen and politicians for centuries. To suggest we are incapable is not merely ludicrous, but racist.

Only in politics – especially in local government - can we say that Scots have performed poorly, and that is only since the Labour hegemony of the last fifty years – and under the Union system.

Scotland should go for a federal system within the UK, getting the best of both worlds

But Scotland is a *nation*, not just another county like Yorkshire or Hampshire, or just another state like Minnesota or Manitoba, or Poitou-Charentes or Lower Saxony.

Countries – normal countries, as an independent Scotland will be – have their own representatives on international bodies such as the United Nations (note: *nations*, not areas or counties or empires) and the European Union, with all their subsidiary bodies, in the Olympics, even in the Eurovision Song Contest. Scotland as Scotland has almost no international presence at all and simply does not contribute as a country among the nations of the earth.

And in a federal system we are forced to follow the economic diktat of a Westminster government whose main interest – quite naturally - is the promotion of London and the South-East, where so many of the population lives. We are also forced to follow 'great power' foreign and defence policies such as Iraq and Trident that may well be anathema to us.

Quite apart from the international dimension, Scotland in a federal Britain would still face the real possibility of time and time again voting for one party and finding itself governed by another. (Of all the seven Tory prime ministers who ruled Scotland for 35 years between 1951 and 1997, only *one* (Eden) ever won an election here – a mandate that lasted for eighteen months before he resigned.)

Scotland would have no clout in Europe or the world – a 'helpless, voiceless bystander'

We have no clout as it is, merely being the poodles of England, as England dominates Westminster with about 85% of the MPs. Just like the other small countries that have had to struggle for independence, an independent Scotland will be realistic about her place in the world, shunning the delusions of grandeur of the British state. Interestingly, we have heard no suggestion that England should become another state of the USA 'to have greater clout'.

Independence or oil or the European Union would not bail Scotland out

We don't need bailed out! Long-term, independence will almost certainly make a fantastic difference. We are not asking to be bailed out by anyone – we want to stand on our own two feet in the same way as other nations do. That what independence means!

Globalisation is best managed by bigger units

That's just not the experience of Europe's small, wealthy nations. Why do the critics not look at such facts?

Why leave a Union that has had such a glorious past?

Empires rise and fall, for good or ill, and history moves on. The British Empire existed over a period of time, again for good or ill, but times have changed. A Union based on sentimental feelings about a glorious past cannot be sustained. Other countries like Holland, Belgium, Norway, Finland, Ireland and Iceland have all taken the same path and have prospered far beyond the forecasts of their former masters. Scotland should follow where they have so successfully led.

And finally – nationalism is bad - it is an outdated nineteenth century philosophy of small-minded separatists

The Scottish National Party wants Scotland to take its place among all the other independent nations of the world, large and small. Do those who criticise the idea of the independence of the Scottish nation launch their savage attacks on other nations such as Norway or Sweden or Denmark. If not, why not? Do they declare that the British state should cease to exist, become one of the states of the United States and be governed from Washington. If not, why not?

In the end, no matter what the arguments, time will change all things. The very fact of the SNP's winning the Scottish elections has transformed the political situation, and many of those who scoffed at the arguments for independence are now more sympathetic to the idea, having seen how an SNP government works. To end with some words from journalist Joyce McMillan:

'… it's obvious to any honest observer that the new crop of SNP ministers – bright, articulate, funny, energetic, and confident enough to be open to new ideas – fit the bill much better than Jack McConnell's outgoing Cabinet, and represent the modern nation much more accurately.'

If that is the change that three months can show, just think what a decade of independence may bring.

" No man has a right to set the bounds to the march of a nation; no man has a right to say to his country, "Thus far shalt thou go and no further".

Charles Stewart Parnell (1846-1891)

Special SI Autumn 2007

CHAPTER 10

The Union and Mr Brown

He talks about British values, innovations and rights

I was quite excited when I heard that Gordon Brown was writing an article laying out the benefits of the Union between England and Scotland,

A real detailed defence of the Union is just what we need so that we can all weigh up the advantages and disadvantages of belonging to Britain.

I was just a bit perturbed when told Mr Brown's article was to be published in the London Daily Telegraph, a newspaper so shunned in Scotland that it is not even taken by a single one of Edinburgh's local public libraries.

So Mr Brown's appeal is aimed in the first instance at English readers and not, as you might expect have expected, at those pesky Scots who are causing all the trouble in the first place.

So what are Prime Minister Brown's great arguments for the Union?

He talks about British values, innovations and rights.

So what are these "values" - "the values we share across the United Kingdom", according to Mr Brown?

Why, they are the values of "liberty, fairness, tolerance, enterprise, civic initiative and internationalism".

Excuse me? Are those not the very values that most advanced nations adhere to and which are better exercised in many other countries than in Britain?

And what are the "innovations" that we have in Britain have benefited from, although "founded" in different parts of the Union – the NHS ("founded by a Welshman"), universal education ("with many of its earliest roots in Scotland") and universal suffrage ("championed by radicals in England").

You would think that other advanced European countries lacked a health service, universal education and universal suffrage.

The truth is, many other countries have health, education and voting systems that are superior to anything we have here.

It is just so much arrogance – so typical and so myopic of Westminster - to claim that we have these benefits because of the Union.

And finally, what are the "rights" we British should be so proud of? Well, for Mr Brown, they are the right to liberty within the law, to education, to healthcare, to help when unemployed and to a state pension!

Gordon, obviously, should get out a bit more. All of these rights are enjoyed by every advanced, civilised country - especially so in the small countries of Scandinavia.

Sadly, Mr Brown's "arguments for the Union" are nothing of the sort. His values are not especially British, his beneficial "innovations" are not peculiar to us and his "rights" are often enjoyed to a greater extent outside Britain.

His article is full of dodgy assertions that simply don't hold up to the most cursory examination. There is really nothing to get your teeth into here.

SI 950 April 2008

CHAPTER 11

How Oldies can help.

Pop down to any by election for an hour or two of leafletting.

So you get to a venerable age. You retire. You have a choice – vegetate, or do something really useful.

Yes, we can still enjoy our holidays. Yes, we can have a great time with our grandchildren. And yes, we may have time to catch up on all those books or 1970s TV series we just didn't have time for because of the pressures of work.

But for us Oldies in the SNP there is really much more that we can contribute. For Oldies can have a terrifically beneficial impact not only on the Party, but also on the public at large.

For one thing, at branch meetings Oldies can be sceptical and controversial and help to develop a critical spirit among the enthusiastic young.

I well remember when I joined Newington Branch in Edinburgh in the 1990s. Stuff came through from headquarters and was enthusiastically endorsed by the younger members.

But three of our senior citizens, Mairi Stewart, Joe Kidd and Ian Dodds, were always around to ask the simple question: 'Why?"

Perhaps not surprisingly, often there was no easy answer. It made people think, which was very good for them.

Quite apart from adding a voice of experience to branch meetings, Oldies are in an ideal position to help out at by-elections. SNP organisation is now often so good – especially if you have access to a computer – that you can easily find out if there is a by-election in your area, contact numbers and times to help out.

Pop down to any by-election - no matter how seemingly unimportant - with a couple of friends for an hour or two for leafletting. It's amazing how much work can be done by two to four leafletters.

And if you enjoy canvassing, so much the better. In the past many people were wary of canvassing, believing that you needed to know a great deal about the intricacies of party policy.

It never was the case, and now it's even less so. Voter identification is best done in a very casual way, and it gives a fascinating insight into how contradictory and irrational human beings can be!

While I have been out in Glasgow East and Glenrothes, there is also the possibility of using the Activate system. I haven't done so myself yet, a friend tells me that it is a piece of cake.

Don't forget, too, that financial donations are vital as well, especially membership contributions, and they are best made by direct debit on a monthly basis.

Did you know that members paying by direct debit rose between 2003 and 2007 from 6.5% to 57.3%, and that members paying through their local branch fell over the same period from 82.7% to 2.5%?

And did you know that over-65s make up 25.4% of SNP membership and that members paying the minimum rate of £12 a year fell from 34.4% to 15.3% in one year, between 2006 and 2007. And that average direct debit payments have risen from £17 to £47 in the last four years?

This reflects just how important Oldies are financially to the SNP.

While the credit crunch is definitely biting, there are still enough of us able to take pleasant holidays to indicate that we can have cash to spare for the SNP!

So all in all, older members of the SNP should not think that their time for helping the party is past. There is so much we can do on a very part-time basis to help us achieve our goal.

SI 957 November 2008

CHAPTER 12

Population density

I'm puzzled by recent assertions that "Britain" is the most densely populated country in Europe.

Here are the relevant figures for EU member states per square km:

Malta	1260
Netherlands	393
Belgium	337
UK	244
Germany	233

However, if by 'Britain', our sloppy journalists mean 'England', a different picture emerges:

England	51,092,000 /130,395 sk = 392 density per sk
Scotland	5,144,200 / 30,414 sk = 65 density per sk
Wales	3,004,600 / 20,779 sk = 140 density per sk
N. Ireland	1,759,000 / 13,843 sk = 122 density per sk

I don't know why the SNP has never made much of the fact that England is more than six times more densely populated than Scotland, with all the strains that that involves. Maybe it's because most of our population is in the central belt – then again, the density in the central belt is probably far below that of London and the South East of England.

And population increase, uncovered while researching representation of MEPs, confirming from different sources the comments from Nick Dekker. (Nick's article in the SI of February 2009 revealed that England has a looming generating gap problem)

I have a 'Book of the World' 1976 edition, which gives interesting population figures (for 1975). The others are for 2007.

Country	1975 (million)	2007 (million)	% change
Austria	7.521	8.170	+8.6
Belgium	9.742	10.275	+5.5
Denmark	5.027	5.369	+10.7
Finland	4.643	5.303	+14.2
Iceland	0.212	0.312	+47.4
Ireland	3.051	4.235	+38.9
Norway	4.030	4.743	+17.7
Sweden	8.138	9.077	+11.6
Switzerland	6.660	7.302	+9.6
United Kingdom	55.968	60.587	+8.3
England	45.900	51.092	+13.1
Wales	2.700	3,004	+11.3
N. Ireland	1.500	1.759	+17.3
Scotland	**5.200**	**5.144**	**-01.1**

A bit of dynamite there: where are our journalists?

SI 962 April 2009

CHAPTER 13

Members of the European Parliament

Under present arrangements Scotland is greatly under-represented

The elections to the European parliament are almost upon us, yet I wonder how many Scots realise just how the British government cheats us out of our proper Scottish allocation of elected members.

Just take a look at the following table. It shows the ten smallest members of the European member states, plus Scotland, with their populations from the smallest to the largest, their number of Euro-MPs and how many Euro-MPs there are for every million of the population.

I have added for the sake of comparison three countries of roughly ten, forty and sixty million, plus Germany, the country with the greatest population in the European Union.

It is worth noting that the European Union recognises that numbers of MEPs should be weighted in favour of less populous countries, as can be clearly seen from the table. The United Kingdom does not apply this rule.

Country	Population (in millions)	Number of MEPs	MEPs per million
Malta	0.4	5	12.50
Luxembourg	0.5	6	12.00
Cyprus	0.8	6	7.50
Estonia	1.3	6	4.61
Slovenia	1.9	7	3.68
Latvia	2.4	8	3.33
Lithuania	3.6	12	3.33
Ireland	4.2	12	2.86
Scotland	**5.1**	**6**	**1.18**
Finland	5.3	13	2.45
Denmark	5.4	13	2.41
Czech Republic	10.3	22	2.13
Poland	38.6	50	1.29
Italy	59.7	72	1.20
Germany	82.2	99	1.2

Does it not seem ludicrous that Scotland, which has more than ten times the population of Luxembourg, should have the same number of MEPs as that tiny 'grand duchy'? Each Scottish MEP has ten times the number of constituents, not to mention vast areas of territory to cover compared with their Luxembourg colleagues. And, further, we used to have 8 MEPs, but over the past few years due to the expansion of the EU, we have been reduced to 6, a drop of 25%.

And with our population of 5.1 million, we actually have fewer MEPs than Slovenia, with its population over 3 million smaller than Scotland's.

Again, Scotland has a population more than one and a half million greater than Lithuania's, yet they have double our number of MEPs.

I think it is fair to say that with our population of more than 5.1 million Scotland is entitled to the 13 MEPs enjoyed by Finland and Denmark, countries that are closest in population to Scotland.

Sadly, it is Westminster that allocates MEP numbers to the individual countries within the United Kingdom. The United Kingdom rejects the European Union idea that there should be a weighting in favour of small countries.

It is truly astonishing when you look at the figures and realise that Germany, by far the largest member of the European, is actually better represented per head of population than Scotland.

In practical terms this all means that Scotland is grossly underrepresented, our MEPs are grossly overworked, are responsible for huge areas compared with other small countries, and there is no chance of a meaningful proportional representational system.

Ireland, for instance, in the last Euro-elections, when it had 13 MEPs, was able to have four constituencies of 4, 3, 3, and 3 MEPs – a far more sensible arrangement.

However, since Scotland is not a member state of the European Union, we do not have an automatic right to be represented on EU institutions such as the European Council, the European Commission, the European Court of Justice, or the European Court of Auditors.

A sad story, indeed.

Scotland as a member state would increase from 6 to 13 MEPs.

Similarly, Wales, between Latvia and Lithuania in population, would increase from 4 to 10, and Northern Ireland, just smaller than Slovenia, would increase from 3 to 7.

England, also, loses out in the current arrangements. Its population of 51.1 would justify an increase from 59 to 61 or 62 – probably the latter, with its increase in population in recent years.

So while the unitary UK has an allocation of 72, if the four states had separate member status, our total would be 61/62+13+10+7 = 91/92 – an increase of 26% or 28%.

Is this a case of 'weaker together, stronger apart!'?

SI Conference Edition Spring 2009

CHAPTER 14
Squandered money

Norway now has an oil fund worth 430 billion dollars

Many folk will remember the terrific hoo-hah there was in the Scottish press when the Scottish Parliament was being built.

Members of the Scottish Parliament were castigated as if they were personally responsible for the overspend.

Not a day went by without some headline assuring us that our MSPs were the lowest of the low and could not run a sweetie shop.

All this in spite of the fact that the major decisions about the building and where it was to be built were taken long before we even elected our MSPs; all decisions were taken by the then Secretary of State for Scotland, Donald Dewar. It was a typical Westminster mess.

Now we are informed that the Westminster Government has quietly dropped its centralisation of the National Health Service computer system; this seems to have been an NHS England project, with perhaps the Welsh getting sucked in, but it is not clear.

Hardly a word of this has appeared in the Scottish press. Yet according to the London Times this attempt has been 'shambolic', 'a spectacular failure'.

The cost has ballooned from an original £2.4 billion to more like £30 billion – more than sixty times the cost of the Scottish Parliament, for a computer system.

Now Chancellor of the Exchequer Alistair Darling has admitted that the system is 'inessential to the frontline.'

It is incredible to think that of all the countries in Europe, apart from Norway, the United Kingdom is the only one to have discovered oil.

Many believed, even about 1975, when the pumps started pumping, that the UK would not make best use of this incredible wealth.

We never realised just how great would be the waste and squandering of that vast income.

First of all, Westminster grabbed the lot for itself, and Scotland was refused any say in how it was spent.

Then they decided that this extraordinary wealth could not possibly be shown in the Scottish statistics, so for the purposes of oil funds they created a new economic 'region' of the British Isles, known as the Continental Shelf from which all the oil wealth flowed.

And as it flowed, this is how they squandered it:

1 Under Mr Callaghan, Britain was in so much debt under Labour that the first tranche was used to pay off borrowings.

2 Under Mrs Thatcher, with huge masses of unemployed, much of the 1980s wealth went on paying unemployment benefit, not to mention the war in the Falklands.

3 Under Mr Blair, Britain went to war more often than under any Prime Minister for more than a century, paying for it with the oil wealth.

4 And of course now, oil wealth is once again being used to bail out a government that by its own lack of prudence helped mightily to bring the present financial crisis on itself.

And now Norway has one of the highest standards of living in the world, and an oil fund worth some $430 billion, while Britain is bankrupt.

SI 972 February 2010 Adapted from the Flag in the Wind

CHAPTER 15
Waste and the Oil Money

What did happen to Scotland's immense oil revenues?

In July 1996 I took a short holiday in Norway, motoring up the West coast from Stavanger to Bergen.

I was immensely impressed by the newly created infrastructure. Once-isolated islands were now linked by new bridges or by tunnels under the sea.

In other areas tunnels through mountains had helped to overcome many of the difficulties presented by Norway's difficult geography.

I commented on this to a Norwegian I met, to which his reply was: "And all done with money from the oil."

Lucky Norway, I thought, to have discovered oil and to have been able to use it sensibly and creatively for the well-being of the Norwegian people.

I was just glad that he didn't ask me how many bridges and tunnels Scotland had built with our oil money.

So what did happen to Scotland's immense oil revenues?

The Early Labour Years

To start with, the Westminster Wilson and Callaghan Labour governments decided Scotland should have no say at all concerning the oil wealth found in Scottish waters.

Then they decided that this extraordinary wealth could not possibly be shown in Scottish statistics as coming from Scotland. That unpleasant truth was politically far too dangerous. So, purely for the purposes of keeping the oil wealth off the Scottish balance sheets, they created a new economic "region" of the British Isles, known as the Continental Shelf from which all the oil wealth was shown to flow.

It is often forgotten that Westminster wanted to extract the oil hell for leather because of the dreadful state of Britain's finances. For years Britain had been underperforming and the crisis finally overtook us in the mid-1970s.

The Callaghan government only managed to raise money from the International Monitory Fund and the much reviled "gnomes of Zürich" by promising that the immense oil wealth which was to come from oil revenues would be used initially to pay back these creditors.

And so it came to pass. Billions of oil revenues saved Britain from a disastrous situation created by its incompetent politicians.

The Conservative Years - Unemployment and War Bills

Mrs Thatcher decided that the British economy was grossly inefficient and needed a shake-out. This was true, up to a point, but her method of shaking out the economy created mass unemployment. The only way Britain was able to pay for this was by using billions of the oil revenues.

An ominous pointer to the future was the spending of oil revenues on the Falklands War. The immediate - as opposed to historic - causes of the war were diplomatic misunderstandings. The Argentinian dictatorship misread British naval actions and thought it had been given the go-ahead for a Falklands takeover. British Foreign Secretary Lord Carrington later honourably resigned over the war.

But Britain was able to finance the war without a second thought because of the wealth pouring into the coffers from oil.

The Blair Years

Under Mr Blair Britain went to war more often than under any prime minister in more than a century. Again, Britain has been able to afford such wars only because of the tremendous wealth coming from the oil.

Especially in Iraq and Afghanistan Britain has spent more money on war than any other European power. Indeed, per head of population, Britain has more troops serving in Afghanistan than any other nation, including the United States!

The Brown Years

It's almost back full circle. Just as James Callaghan used future oil wealth to bail out Britain in the 1970s, so Gordon Brown will be using the oil wealth to bail out Britain from now on. A heavy price will be exacted for Gordon Brown's lack of prudence.

Brown's "light-touch" regulation enabled banks to cast off their traditional prudence and led ultimately to their collapse. Their reckless lending patterns led to a property bubble and a mountain of bad debts.

Brown's lack of interest in or blindness to the excesses of the City of London led to wage excess throughout Britain, even in some areas of the public sector.

The results of the inevitable crash will be with us for years to come and once more oil revenues will be used to pay for the folly of our politicians.

Investing for the Future

The Westminster government has not invested any oil wealth in funds for the future.

By contrast, in 1990 the Norwegian government created a new Sovereign Wealth Fund for the future. Last September it stood at £259 billion (that for a country of under 5 million!). It owns more than 1 per cent of the entire world's shares. It is Europe's biggest equity investor. It is one of the world's three largest sovereign wealth funds.

Little Norway can feel very proud of the way its governments have so sensibly managed its vast oil revenues.

We should feel ashamed of the squandering of our own vast oil resources and at being conned by Westminster politicians and their friends into allowing it.

SI Spring Edition 2010

CHAPTER 16

How to win friends –
south of the Border

It's about time we stood up and declared these truths loud and clear.

It seems that Tory leader in London David Cameron wants to shake up the 1970s Barnett formula by which, it is claimed, the Scots get 20 per cent more money per head than the English.

Now that's a funny thing. If this is true, then it seems that in the 1970s Barnett found that the so-called benefits of belonging to the United Kingdom had left the Scottish population needing 20 per cent more cash than the English!

Incredible! While countries such as Denmark, Norway, Sweden and Finland have all managed to survive very well on their own, we apparently need to be subsidised! After more than 270 years of so-called benefits, Scotland could not even sustain its relatively low standard of living without subsidies! We can't even stand on our own two feet.

At this point you may well want to pose some questions. (1) Who on earth, you may ask yourself, was responsible for this incredible state of affairs? (2) What political system allowed this to happen? (3) What political party failed Scotland so badly?

Well, the short answers are (1) the political Union that left Scotland without control of her own affairs is responsible: even now, we are dragged into an illegal war, squandering money on it and having our soldiers killed in it; (2) the Westminster political system that leaves the Scottish population mostly on the sidelines with governments we never voted for – six out of the seven Tory prime ministers between 1951 and 1997 never won an election in Scotland; (3) all London-based political parties have failed Scotland - as soon as they were elected they have turned their backs on promised modernising reforms.

It's about time that we stood up and declared these truths loud and clear. It sometimes seems that with all the spin and trivia in the media we fail to see the very basics of what makes a country prosper.

Now if David Cameron wants a review of the Barnett formula, what is to stop the Scottish government commissioning a Report by a small group of eminent Scottish economists, entitled, say, *The Use and Abuse of Oil Revenue?*

First of all, the Report would look at oil revenue historically and examine the claims made by the British Labour and Conservative governments of the time of the amount of oil that could be extracted and the expected revenue, and contrast that with Scottish National Party statistics of the time.

Secondly, the Report could study the oil analyses available to the British governments of the time, examine why and to what extent the results were either ignored, distorted or suppressed by those British governments.

Thirdly, the Report could look into how many billions of oil revenue were squandered to cover for the economic incompetence of Labour and Conservative governments, 1966 to 1979.

Fourthly, it could analyse the billions of oil revenue spent by incompetent Conservative governments (a) to cover massive increases in unemployment benefit and (b) to prop up sterling in the early 1990s.

Fifthly, the Report could look into the billions of pounds spent by Labour governments on wars since 1997, and especially the illegal Iraq war, the reasons for which as we know are founded on lies.

Sixthly, the Report could analyse how Norway managed to use its billions of oil revenue on massive infrastructure improvements and just how Norway has succeeded in saving billions of pounds of oil revenue for future generations.

There may well be other aspects that an oil commission could look at but the above six areas should do for starters.

And as for Britain's ludicrous first-past-the-post voting system, on the other side of the political divide, Gordon Brown has never, ever, shown any inclination to change it. Indeed, in the past he has actively opposed such a move.

Just before the 1997 general election, when it looked as if Tony Blair might need Liberal Democratic support to govern Labour promised to look into the question of a different voting system.

As it turned out Labour did not need the LibDems, and the promise was dropped.

And for twelve years Labour never considered the idea again.

Now, all of a sudden, Brown comes up with the carrot of a referendum on a voting system called the Alternative Vote. But the people will not be asked to consider the fairest and most democratically representative system (STV – Single Transferable Vote), but rather a system that may well lead to even more distorted results than at present.

Brown hopes that this offer will attract enough middle of the road voters to vote Labour to keep the Tories out of power. It is a cynical ploy.

But again, while it may be a cynical ploy, it may just be that this will at last bring the voting system to the front of people's minds and help to bring about change that has been needed for a century.

It will be interesting to see.

SI 975 May 2010

This article was adapted from the Flag in the Wind; it was written before the beauty contest that was the Leaders Debates focussed attention on the Liberal Democrats.

CHAPTER 17

Tony Blair's 1999 North Sea Grab

Annexation - the so-called Scottish Adjacent Waters Boundaries Order 1999

The spring of 1999 was an exciting time for Scotland. Two years before, in June, 1997, the Labour party had won a landslide victory; and just four months later, in September 1997, the Scottish people had voted in a historic referendum for a new devolved Scottish Parliament at Holyrood, in Edinburgh.

Parties had been choosing candidates for Holyrood seats and regional lists, and a new site, architect and design for the parliament building were being chosen.

The peak of electioneering was reached in March and April of 1999 in preparation for the elections on Thursday 6 May, 1999.

Naturally, many Scottish MPs who were standing in the elections for Holyrood, came back to Scotland to campaign. It is likely that at no period in the history of the UK parliament had so few Scottish MPs been left in Westminster to defend Scotland's interests.

From the middle of March and for the next six weeks the Scottish media were taken up with reporting all the ins and outs of the Scottish campaign.

From the London media came a daily barrage of news about the horrific war in Yugoslavia.

Over the entire duration of the Scottish election campaign images of refugees, bombings and war dominated television news.

As someone once said in another context, this was a great time to bury bad news.

And the bad news for Scotland was that some 6,000 thousand square miles of its territorial waters had just been grabbed by the Westminster government.

Here's what happened.

In 1968, the UK government set the border latitude at 55°50' N by the Continental Shelf (Jurisdiction) Order 1968. This Order acknowledged Scottish marine jurisdiction north of this border line of latitude which lies east-west just north of Berwick on Tweed. This was also the line to which the Scottish Fisheries Cruisers operated.

However, on April 13, 1999, just over two weeks before the Scottish Parliament was elected, a strange thing happened. The UK government unilaterally changed this fishing boundary, thereby annexing some 6,000 square miles of Scottish waters (also rich in oil and gas) and transferring them from the original international boundary into English jurisdiction.

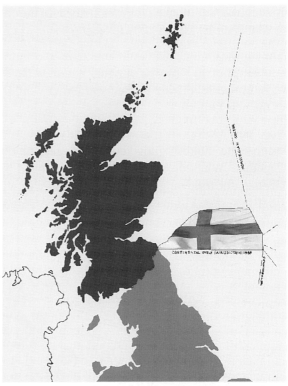

The grab - in black and white, or Westminster grey?

This annexation was imposed by the so-called Scottish Adjacent Waters Boundaries Order 1999.

According to The Herald newspaper (23 May 1999) this Order 'was passed by the House of Lords and the Committee on Delegated Legislation on March 23, but was not openly debated in the Commons ... a Scottish Office spokesman said the change in the fishing boundary - which did not come to light until early last week [i.e. two months after it was passed by the House of Lords] - was necessary as a result of Scottish devolution (but) he could not explain the constitutional logic of the boundary alteration.'

When questioned, a Scottish Office spokesman made the strange claim that 'full and proper parliamentary procedures were followed'.

All very strange. So strange, indeed, that Richard Lochhead MSP decided to find out more. He submitted a Freedom of Information Act request to the Scotland Office on 9 March 2005 asking for all relevant papers and correspondence in connection with the Order.

His request was blocked for four years until the documents were finally made available on 10 March 2009 (except for some 'redactions', i.e. censorship).

The excuse for the delay was that the UK government was and is giving active consideration to a new draft Order based on the 1999 Order and that release of information relating to the 1999 Order would prejudice the development of the new Order.

The 'new Order' will almost certainly go beyond fishing boundaries and incorporate English jurisdiction and annexation over oil, gas and other minerals. When the relevant chart was plotted by a retired Merchant Navy Captain, the following oil wells close to the Norwegian boundary fell into the English sector: Fulmar, Auk, Clyde, Janice, Angus and Fife. Their pipeline runs to St Fergus in Aberdeenshire.

Special Edition Summer 2010.

CHAPTER 18
What to do about the lies?

It always comes as a surprise to decent, ordinary folk to realise just how blatant and shameless political liars can be.

Joan McApine in the Sunday Times of 9 May 2010 had an outstanding article titled "Murphy's Big Lie is still working".

She first pointed out that Labour's campaign had been aimed at keeping the Tories out of government. When this was achieved Labour turned round and claimed that the election result was "a verdict on the SNP government". As Ms McAlpine commented: "They all knew that it was nothing of the kind."

She then pointed out that Murphy accused Salmond of "planning a deal with the Tories". As she said: This is untrue ... It is also (SNP) party policy not to strike alliances with the Conservatives".

This did not stop Labour MP David Cairns from saying: "(They (the SNP) must be cooking up a deal with the Tories."

Ms McAlpine adds more about this lie and its technique. "It's absurd and Labour knows this. So why? You could call it Scottish Labour's Big Lie, the propaganda technique where you choose a lie so audacious the public think you would not dare make it up. Then you repeat it continually until they believe it."

And of course, if you deny the lie, then the lie itself gains a momentum of its own.

It's sad, but true. Other lies I have noticed in the past year have included "SNP cuts in Scotland" which are in fact Labour Westminster cuts (Westminster controls the money), the SNP is anti-Glasgow (because there was no money for the airport link) while it was the Labour opposition that had voted to spend incredible sums on a small Edinburgh tram line – against the wishes of the SNP government.

These of course are the most blatant, political lies which are trotted at times of crisis. The biggest running lie is: "The union has been good for Scotland."

You only need to take a look over the years to see that the statistics prove otherwise. It is the small countries of northern Europe that in general lead our continent and the world in almost every area you would wish to nominate.

SI 976 June 2010 : this article was first published in the Flag in the Wind

CHAPTER 19

No coincidences

It was a dramatic moment when on Thursday May 3, 2007, the leader of the Scottish National Party Alex Salmond led his party to victory and went on to form the first SNP government in Scottish history.

British Prime Minister Gordon Brown was so incensed at the result that he tried to cajole his Scottish Labour leader into forming an alliance with the Liberal Democrats to thwart the winning party.

Fortunately Brown failed. But for weeks he famously took a fit of the sulks and could not bring himself even to congratulate Scotland's new First Minister.

Sadly this little episode tells you a great deal about Gordon Brown and his unwillingness to face up to reality.

But the result of that election in May 2007 was also a warning to the London political establishment: if you leave the Scots to a political debate amongst themselves, London may well get an unpleasant surprise.

The upshot of all this has so far has been threefold. The London political establishment has decided that the Scottish independence movement must be prevented at all cost from putting over without outside interference their independence message.

Firstly, in the British general election of May 2010 Scotland's largest and governing party was totally excluded from the televised debates beamed from London throughout Britain, including Scotland.

This in turn led to the Scottish National Party being almost completely excluded from the follow-up news and discussion programmes, and of course from the extensive coverage in the press. London-based politicians were identified in the mind of the public as the only real contenders in the election, with predictable results for the other parties based outside the English capital.

That was the first scandal.

Secondly, it has now been decided by the new Conservative/Liberal Democrat coalition to hold a referendum on the voting system – on the very day in May 2011 that voters in Scotland will be going to the polls to decide on the next Scottish government.

Once again, of course, during the weeks before the Scottish election the television news (almost all based in London) and the press coverage will be dominated by London politicians. What a harvest of publicity the London-dominated media will give to the London-dominated parties.

That will be the second scandal.

And finally, of course, the new coalition has decided to hold the next British general election in May 2015 – again, on the very day that the Scots go to the polls to choose their government.

Once again, the media will be dominated by propaganda from London, and all the Scottish arguments will be submerged under blethers from down south.

That is the third scandal.

And none of it is coincidence.

SI 978 August 2010. This was first published in The Flag in the Wind.

CHAPTER 20
The hunt for real news

So like so many others I shall probably give up on newspapers altogether.

One of the saddest spectacles in Scotland these days is that of the serious intelligent and decent Scot in search of a serious intelligent and decent newspaper.

I am beginning to meet many friends who have abandoned their newspaper of a lifetime and who are roaming around, trying a new paper for a few months, then trying another, then having a rest from any before starting the hunt again.

I myself had the *Herald* newspaper that came into my parents' home and then mine for more than sixty years. Such a habit is not broken easily, but last December I stopped taking the *Herald* for the first time in my life.

Why? It had nothing whatsoever to do with the major reason normally put forward for falling newspaper circulation – the internet.

No, I simply got fed up with the dishonesty and tendentious reporting that the *Herald* had resorted to.

The same thing had happened to the *Scotsman*. I had started reading the Edinburgh-based paper in the seventies, when the *Scotsman* really sparkled. It was great fun to read and really made you think.

After a really serious falling away in the eighties under editor Magnus Linklater I finally gave up on it in the early nineties. As I say, it takes a long time and something seriously adrift for a reader to leave a newspaper.

Since then I have tried to give the *Scotsman* a chance, buying it once every three months or so, but it has always proved to be pretty pathetic.

More recently I thought its editorials showed signs of improvement so I decided to try out a deal for some three months. The three months were up in September, and alas, I did not renew. If anything, the reporting has become even worse. The main political correspondent is a mere cynical political propagandist. His articles, if they can be classed as journalism at all, are of a very poor standard.

Much of the so-called news is a farrago of nonsense. Negativity reigns supreme. Like many others, I have just had enough of starting my day off with such nonsense at breakfast every morning.

So where to go now? I have tried the so-called *Scottish Daily Mail* and the

Scottish Daily Express, neither of which has a Scottish website (now there's a give-away). The *Mail* in particular is a vicious, nasty paper intent on making its readers as angry as possible. Its favourite headline word seems to be "outrage". It's not that its readers have ever had the time to be outraged about a breaking news story, it's just that the *Mail* tells them that outrage is the expected reaction.

As for the poor old *Daily Record*, it's a long time since it could ever be taken seriously.

Last year my search took me to the London *Times*, which at least was recognisably a newspaper with real rather than invented news. It's not bad, and if I lived in England it might be a serious contender.

Sadly, I have never really been able to get into the *Guardian*, although I feel it should be the sort of paper I would be most at home with.

No, that honour goes to *The Independent*, which seems to me to be by far the most intelligent, balanced and decent newspaper in Britain today. Sadly, its coverage of Scottish news lets it down, so like so many others I shall probably give up on newspapers altogether.

Meanwhile, for decent discussion there is Kenneth Roy's excellent *Scottish Review* on the internet, and for world coverage the first-rate *The Week*.

It's beginning to look as if the Scottish newspapers are beyond help, and we'll just have to wait until they collapse and may be reborn from the awful ashes.

SI 980 October 2010

This article was first published in the Flag in the Wind, and then on newsnetscotland. www.newsnetscotland.com

CHAPTER 21
Scotland Squeezed

So Scotland's wings had to be clipped – But how?

When Winifred Ewing took her seat as member of the European Parliament (MEP) in June 1975 she was the first Scottish politician to represent Scotland directly, as a nation, among other nations, in almost three hundred years.

The British establishment did not like that one little bit.

The fact that Winnie was feisty, intelligent, witty, articulate, charismatic and got on very well with MEPs from other countries only made matters worse from Westminster's point of view.

So Scotland's wings had to be clipped. But how?

First of all, Scotland's position as a mere region of the UK, and not a country, had to be confirmed. That's one of the reasons London has cut our EU representation twice in the last decade to less than half of Ireland's. For further details, see below.

British governments also feel a need to ensure that Scotland has as low an international profile as possible.

Here are just a couple of examples.

Vote ignored by Gordon Brown

Some time ago it was decided by a vote at a meeting of the Council of the Isles (consisting of First Ministers and their Deputies from Scotland, Wales and Northern Ireland, Prime Ministers of Ireland and the Isle of Man, plus a representative of the UK government) that the Council's Secretariat should be based in Edinburgh.

Gordon Brown was Prime Minister at the time and decided unilaterally that he would ignore the vote. Unfortunately for him, news of his high-handed attitude reached the press and did not do poor Brown's reputation any good at all.

Fortunately, Gordon has gone and the original decision to base the Secretariat in Edinburgh now stands once more.

Scottish Fishing Secretary Squeezed Out

This mirrored another incident at a Fisheries Meeting in Brussels when a British Minister had to return to the UK and a civil servant had been instructed to occupy his chair for the rest of the meeting to prevent the Scottish Fisheries Secretary Richard Lochhead taking his place!

But Not This Time!

And just at the end of September the new British government was wanting farming Minister Jim Paice MP - who has no portfolio role on fisheries - to lead a UK delegation in Brussels on the thorny issue of mackerel quotas.

After a strong and well-argued letter to David Cameron from Alex Salmond, pointing out that Scotland's share of the UK's quota and landings in this instance is 90%, the UK government backed down and Richard Lochhead spoke on the issue.

Gross Under-representation

The European Union clearly shows the vital necessity for a country - any country - to be independent in the modern world. For there is a dramatic difference in influence between those countries, even the smallest, that run their own affairs, and those that do not.

Take the simple matter of representation in the EU.

Scotland has a population of 5.2 million. The Westminster parliament allows us to have just six European Members of the European Parliament (MEPs).

There are three other countries - Denmark, Finland and Slovakia - that, like Scotland, have just over five million inhabitants. They, however, are independent, so they get more than double our score, with 13 representatives each.

Even more shocking is the fact that three countries - Cyprus, Luxembourg and Malta - all have populations of less than one million, yet they all have six members of the European parliament, the same as Scotland.

In fact, Scotland has 13 times the population of Malta, yet still has the same number of Euro-MPs!

And it's not just Scotland that suffers.

Wales, too, because it has to take its orders from London, is also grossly disenfranchised. Instead of having about 10 MEPs, it has a mere four.

Interestingly, in the European Union, independent countries, no matter how small, must have at least six MEPs. In the entire European Union, Wales is the only country that comes in below that number, although Scotland is definitely at risk if London decides to squeeze us again.

SI Conference issue October 2010

CHAPTER 22
Madame Ecosse – s'il vous plait

Round and About

I often feel that the Party should choose venues in the central belt from time, just to show that we are a party of the whole of Scotland.

Why not Edinburgh or Glasgow or a return to Motherwell? Or Dumfries or Galashiels or even a return to Ayr, of fond memory?

Yes, I know there could be problems of accommodation in the smaller towns, and financial implications in the larger, but all the same - has the Party *really* tried?

But even I must admit that it's hard to beat Inverness or Perth on a fine October day, with their open spaces, autumnal trees and walks along the rivers.

And Perth this year was just superb. Crisp and fine and over the entire four days, not a hint of rain.

For me these days, the conference carries multiple joys. Eating with friends, meeting up with older friends from around Scotland, banter at the Scots Independent stall. I was even persuaded to take out two subscriptions to the new *Independence* magazine and the parliamentary *Holyrood* magazine. Am I going soft in my old age?

The Nitty Gritty

Two things struck me forcibly this year, inside the hall and on the fringe.

In the conference hall itself, the major set speeches by people like John Swinney, Kenny MacAskill, Nicola Sturgeon and Alex Salmond were all excellent, as we have come to expect. Many other speeches were more than competent.

But when it came to the various resolutions, why are we playing it all so safe nowadays? One after another, resolutions were 'passed by acclaim'. Few even had amendments, and even when they did, these were non-controversial.

Granted, we don't want to knock lumps out of each other - especially in front of the cameras. But it would make for a better and livelier conference if things were a bit less anodyne, if delegates really had some tougher meat to chew on.

And finally, as far as the official part was concerned, while the new party political broadcast is excellent did we really have to hear it quite so often. It began to seem like time-filling, if not quite time-wasting.

Two Fringe Highlights

For me, there were two highlights of the fringe - and the first I did not even get to see because of an annoying clash of times.

Christine Grahame MSP had succeeded in getting hold of the prize-winning Dutch-made investigative TV documentary *Lockerbie Revisited*.

This proved so popular that it had to have two showings to packed audiences. It has still never been shown in Britain, a devastating comment on the pusillanimous placemen at the top of the BBC.

Then there was the *Scots Independent* reception. Ian Hamilton, Business Manager of the SI had managed to acquire the BBC Alba documentary *Madame Ecosse*, the story of Winnie Ewing and the rise of the SNP in the second half of the twentieth century.

What a wonderful documentary! What a fantastic woman! The film brought back afresh so many memories and taught so many lessons. As time goes by, you tend to forget just how remarkable Winnie is.

SNP Euro
candidates for the 1984
European Election at Strasbourg. Left to right:
Dan Hood , Janette Jones, Dr David Stevenson, Norman MacLeod,
George Leslie, Jenny Heriot and Ian Goldie, with Winnie Ewing, Madame Ecosse

A marvellous campaigner, she took the incredibly safe Hamilton seat from Labour in November 1967. In February 1974 she defeated the sitting Secretary of State for Scotland Gordon Campbell to take Moray and Nairn. In 1979, against all odds and newspaper predictions, she defeated the Liberal Russell Johnstone to take the Highlands and Islands Euro-seat and went on to hold it for twenty years.

And in 1999 she was elected to the Scottish Parliament and as the oldest member opened the proceedings with the memorable words: 'The Scottish Parliament, adjourned on the 25th day of March in the year 1707, is hereby reconvened.'

(Apparently it was Dr Robert MacIntyre, shortly before his death in February 1998 and just a year before elections to the Parliament, who asked her to use those words.)

What particularly struck me about *Madame Ecosse* was the footage of Winnie arguing her case in the European Parliament. Here was film of a tremendous political performer - passionate, humorous, convinced and convincing. I was amazed that such footage existed.

Had this been shown on television news during those years of her activity in Europe - even just for one minute a month - not only would it have enhanced the stature of Winnie and the SNP during some dark years, but also it would have educated the public about the importance of political developments in the European Community.

But then we never did get to see such wonderful stuff. I wonder why?

SI 981 November 2010

CHAPTER 23

Human Development Index - Britain in Context

But it's not just in the small everyday matters that Norway is impressive.

Short Visit to Norway

My son is married to a Norwegian girl and I paid a short four-day visit to see him and his family at the end of October.

How pleasant it was to arrive in a country where the airport is served by a railway just a couple of hundred yards away from the terminal.

And then to find that as British pensioners we only had to pay half the normal fare on trains.

But it's not just in the small everyday matters that Norway is impressive.

Norway is impressive because its politicians have been wise and farsighted. They have made - mostly - good decisions, based on a realistic view of their country.

They have used the tremendous opportunities offered by its oil wealth to pay off debts, build a previously unimaginable transport infrastructure, create a superb social structure - and then go on to build a fund for future generations totalling at present more than £300 billion.

So it comes as no surprise to find that two recent reports have shown that Norway is not only just about the richest country in the world (again), but it uses that oil wealth to give its people the highest standard of living in the world (again).

HDI -The Big Picture

While it is no doubt great to feel that you belong to the richest country in the world, the real test of a country is how its wealth is distributed and how well the general population is treated.

That is where the HDI (Human Development Index), published by the United Nations, comes in. It is a much more sophisticated attempt to assess a country overall.

The latest HDI was published in November. It covers most countries in the world, but for the sake of comparison I'll concentrate mostly on our European neighbours.

The top ten places are Norway, Australia, New Zealand, USA, Ireland, Liechtenstein, Netherlands, Canada, Sweden and Germany.

Interestingly, from a Scottish point of view, is that half of these countries have fewer than ten million of a population.

Again, it is fascinating to learn that Japan, after - according to the experts - some twenty years of stagnation - still manages to come in at eleventh position, and South Korea rises to twelfth. (in 1998 South Korea came 30th.)

The United Kingdom comes in at 26th, below every other major western European country, save Portugal. (Andorra, Malta and Cyprus also come below Britain.)

The United Kingdom is now closely pursued by three former Communist Eastern Bloc countries: Czech Republic (28th), Slovenia (29th), and Slovakia (31st).

How sad, and incredible, it is to see Britain sink to this level. For these former Communist countries started off just twenty years ago at levels far below us. And of course, none of them had the apparent benefit of having billions of pounds pumped into their economies.

HDI - Some Fascinating Details

The overall picture of Britain's decline compared with other nations is worrying enough. But it is in some of the detail that not just decline but downright decadence becomes apparent.

To arrive at a balanced picture, the HDI takes into account seven areas. These are: Health, Education, Income, Inequality, Gender, Sustainability and Human Security.

It is the overall picture that is important.

And what we find is that in general the United Kingdom spends less of its wealth on health and education than most other Western European countries.

Our overall average income per person is lower than most, but not dramatically so. (Although that 'average' hides greater inequality than most.)

But it is the hard facts of life as it is lived that Britain really, really, suffers. The inequalities in education, life expectation, and gender are more striking than in most other Western countries.

Savings, correctly, comes under the Sustainability section in the HDI report. Britain's net savings (by Gross National Income - GNI) come to 3.9%, compared with Norway's 16.2%, Sweden's 20.5% and Germany's 15.7%. This does not bode well for the future.

Finally, and perhaps most strikingly, is the section headed Human Security.

Here we have such areas as unemployment, homicide and robbery.

While unemployment rates vary considerably, it is in general the smaller countries that have the lower rates and the larger ones that have the higher ones.

Homicide and robbery rates are shown per 100,000 inhabitants.

At a rate of 4.8, Britain's homicide rate is four to five times greater than most.

And with a robbery rate of 281.8, we compare very badly with Norway (33.5), Sweden (96.8) and Germany (60.7).

These, then, are my first thoughts on the HDI report published in the second week in November.

The overall picture is fascinating and there are some fascinating facts, and anomalies, in the detailed country reports.

SI 982 December 2010

CHAPTER 24

Media ignores the Independence debate

SNP government has been grievously thwarted by cynical politicking.

In a fascinating article on the front page of last month's Scots Independent Gordon Wilson wrote of the strange contradiction in the progress made by the Scottish Independence movement over the last 55 years. From being a small almost unknown party in the 1950s, the SNP has now had a continual presence in Westminster since 1967. Through our efforts and the danger we posed to the London parties, the Scottish Parliament was created in 1999, and the SNP formed the first nationalist government ever in 2007.

But as Gordon says: *It is not enough.*

We still do not have independence and support lags around one third of our people.

Why this is so - the current debate

Scottish political discussion at the moment is dominated by three areas.

The first - and most striking but superficial - is the continuing conflict at the Holyrood Parliament. The good work is done quietly in committees, but the public sees the Punch and Judy knockabout which is First Minister's Questions and - apart from political anoraks - becomes bored and switches off.

The second is the implementation of policy. The SNP minority has governed better than anyone could have hoped. It has brought in many long-awaited common-sense measures.

But it has also been grievously thwarted by cynical politicking.

The third area is the media commentary on the SNP government. Many of the best, most progressive and humane measures have led to ferocious and cynical media criticism. The attempt to make a start on combating Scotland's huge alcohol problem, sensible measures of prison reform, the compassionate release of a probably innocent and certainly dying Al-Megrahi - all have been used by a not only insincere and cynical tripartite opposition in parliament but also by a deceitful Scottish media determined to undermine the Scottish government.

The debate that's missing

Once again, Gordon Wilson hits the nail on the head. Our primary weakness is the low level of support for independence. He criticises the Party for having *prioritised its role in government and devoted little of its resources towards presenting a relevant, modern economic case for independence.*

I go along with that, while I understand the huge difficulties we face in getting our message across. But why concentrate on just the economic case?

It's the overall debate about independence that is missing almost completely from the Scottish media.

Yes, most people want to be reassured that they will be at least no worse off come independence.

But economics is not the issue to set the heart racing. It is when people feel that they are being cheated, lied to, conned, manipulated, governed by incompetent and out-of-touch cynics that they begin, in anger, to look elsewhere.

And if a political party can present a vision for a better society and convey that vision to the people then it will make a start on winning the argument.

Elements of the vision we should promote

Only with independence can we escape from the decadent British system.

We must stand for a fairer and more just society. British society has become less fair and less just in recent years. No Westminster party has made any long-term difference.

We must reform our political system. The British political system is broken. Far too many of our MPs are of poor calibre and self-seeking. And for more than 70,000 voters to be represented by one incompetent MP is a scandal.

We must reform our democracy. In fact, it is stretching the imagination to call our system a democracy, especially if you live in Scotland. From 1951 to 1997 - almost half a century, Scotland was ruled for almost 70% of the time by a Conservative Party we never voted for - Churchill, Macmillan, Home, Heath, Thatcher and Major never won an election in Scotland.

We must abandon the delusions and great-power mentality of Westminster politicians and London journalists. In the end reality will always beat delusion hands down.

The nation of Scotland must find and take its own place along with other normal countries.

We must at all times try to instil a true spirit of independence and resilience in the people. Standing on our own two feet brings responsibility and with it dignity.

We must fight the attempt to make Scots feel that only they are incompetent to run their own affairs, only they have to hold out a scrounging begging bowl.

And we must show how Scottish attitudes, the realistic attitudes of the people of a small country, are very different from the attitudes of a former world power still desperate to prove to itself that it remains a major world force in 21st century.

And finally we must confront the so-called *Union dividend* and with every fact at out disposal show what a complete nonsense it is.

SI 983 January 2011

CHAPTER 25

The Scottish System We Will Change

Vast oil revenues have been stolen from Scotland and squandered for decades.

OK, with independence we want a new Scotland. So what should be our basic ideas?

If you build on an old edifice, you have to pull down before you build up.

So with independence, what will we pull down? What do we have to get rid of from the old British state before we can build anew?

Historical

Historically, The Union of the Crowns in 1603 meant that Scotland was left without its own resident king or court. The centre of power upped and moved 400 miles beyond the border, with all that that meant for political and cultural life.

With the Union of the Parliaments in 1707, the national governing body, such as it was, was decapitated.

With almost no political recourse, this was one of the major factors in the clearances of the highlands and islands, vast emigration over the following two centuries, and the incredible number of deaths of young Scots over the following three centuries as they fought for Britain, established the British Empire, sought to hold it together, fought the French as they threatened the British, and in World War I fought off German attempts at empire building.

With independence, all this will change.

The Current Situation
Outdated Political Institutions

For a start, of course, our political institutions will have to change dramatically.

At the moment, our MPs are based 400 miles beyond our borders. They spend most of their working lives outside the country on whose behalf they are legislating. Our Scottish MPs make up less than ten per cent of all MPs in London. They spend most of their time dealing with English matters rather than Scottish. And it has shown - up until devolution - in the neglect over decades of some of Scotland's most pressing problems.

All that will change

Distorted Voting System

At the moment, Scotland more often than not elects a majority from one party, and has to put up with being ruled by another. Or, as in the present instance, being governed not by the winning party or majority, by the two parties - Tories and LibDems - that came last in the general election.

Not only that, we have to work with an electoral system - first-past-the-post - the effect of which grossly distorts the real result of the vote and the wishes of the people.

Another consequence of this iniquitous system is to reinforce a political caricature of different parts of Britain.

All this will change.

The 'Great Power' Mentality

Worse than all this, our Scottish MPs have to work in a parliament that cannot accept that Britain is no longer a great power. That is why Britain retains at enormous cost its nuclear weapons, why it possesses at enormous cost Trident nuclear submarines [based on the Clyde (a prime target so close to a huge centre of population)], and why Britain continues to fight wars and lose young lives across the globe.

This assumption - chiefly by politicians, the media and in the south-east of England - that Britain is still a great power, this belief in Britain's superiority, this arrogance towards foreigners - all this leads to Britain being held world-wide in much lower esteem than its general population deserves.

This disdain of foreigners has a parallel in a contempt, expressed mostly in the London-based media, for Scots in general. Virulent articles in the press, and the scorn expressed by such as Baroness Deech last year, have no parallel in Scotland.

Scotland's Lowly Place

Moreover, because Scotland has less than nine per cent of the British population, we have very little clout. Almost always, if Scotland's interest interests are opposed to England's, then England's interests win. In a British context, that is only common sense.

Not only is Scotland's population less than ten per cent of Britain's, it is much more wide-spread. Population density in England is about 375 per square kilometre, while in Scotland it is only 66. This means that England is one of the most densely populated countries in Europe, but that Scotland is one of the least.

So of course, if you form the government in the south of England, it makes very good sense to site nuclear submarines far from England's centres of population.

It makes sense to site the original nuclear power plant Windscale (later changed to Sellafield, its reputation was so poor) in the far north-west of England, so that any contamination that leaks into the sea will be carried by currents, not south, but north away from England along the Scottish coast and round into the North Sea. (And while no Scottish Tory MP was willing to criticise this, the Norwegian government made its concerns clear to Mrs Thatcher in the 1980s.)

It makes sense to dump toxic waste in the Irish Sea.

It makes sense to site Trident nuclear submarines on the Clyde, even although they may well be a prime target at the beginning of any major war.

It makes sense to practice as much low flying as possible through Scotland's glens and over our mountains.

All this will change.

Exploitation of Scottish Resources

But it is not only our land area, and our young men who have been exploited in an attempt to maintain Britain's unattainable ambitions, it is our physical resources that have recently and most obviously been abused by the British state.

In the 1970s, our fishing industry was used by the Heath government as a mere tool to ease us into the then Common Market. The Scots were not asked, but the industry was sold down the river.

And again in the 1970s, with dreadful and continuing consequences, vast oil revenues have been stolen from Scotland and squandered for decades.

All these things must change. They are all very physical and obvious.

What above all must change are the negative attitudes that have been instilled into Scots for generations since 1707. Now that's a real challenge.

SI 984 February 2011

CHAPTER 26

Our Soundest Argument - International Comparisons

Our unionist-controlled media just cannot accept publication of these facts.

While the SNP government at Holyrood has governed well and morally over the past four years, and has implemented many of its policies, I still find a reluctance among all too many Scots to believe that Scotland can succeed as an independent nation.

This negativity might have been acceptable forty years ago, when international comparisons over decades were not available.

But it is totally unacceptable now. For we have international facts and comparisons that highlight just how well small countries in northern Europe perform against any international criteria.

I believe it is time to hit the population very hard with some of these indubitable facts - facts that show that it is the small countries of northern Europe that are among the wealthiest, the fairest, and the best governed in the world.

While the majority of these small countries perform incredibly well, facts highlighting this are striking by their almost total absence from Scottish media. Our unionist-controlled media just cannot accept publication of these facts, let alone discussion of them.

Historical Perspective

After the slaughter, chaos and turmoil of the Second World War, it took Europe between fifteen and twenty years to regain a pattern of economic growth and political stability.

Even in 1961, the richest six countries per head were still those that, while involved in the war one way or another, had not suffered invasion (apart from Luxembourg).

The Basic Fact - Small Countries Do Well

(OECD statistics: GDP per head - countries with under 11 million population are in **bold**.)

1961 GDP per head:

1 USA 2 Canada 3 **Sweden** 4 **Switzerland** 5 **New Zealand** 6 **Luxembourg**

They were followed by Australia, West Germany, Britain and France.

Britain was in 9th position, **Norway** in 12th, and **Ireland** in 19th. Ireland had a mere 47% of Britain's GDP per head.

Ten years later the situation had become a bit clearer, with some of the countries that had suffered badly during the war making great strides.

1971 GDP per head:

1 USA 2 **Sweden** 3 Canada 4 **Switzerland** 5 West Germany 6 **Denmark**

By 1971, Britain was in 15th place, and had been leap-frogged by **Belgium** and the Netherlands. Norway had climbed to 8th, with **Ireland** still in 20th, but now with 61% of Britain's GDP per head.

Fast forward almost forty years to the very latest figures (2009) produced by the World Bank for OECD countries, and what do we find?

2009 GDP per head:

1 **Luxembourg** 2 **Norway** 3 **Switzerland** 4 **Denmark** 5 **Ireland** 6
Netherlands
7 USA 8 **Austria** 9 **Finland** 10 **Sweden** 11 **Belgium** 12 Australia

In other words, the five richest nations by GDP per head (all European), all have populations of under 8 million. And of the top twelve, nine have populations under 11 million.

So the facts show that over decades the small countries have consistently outperformed the larger.

But what about Ireland? and Iceland?

It is quite true that most countries, for various reasons, hit problems at some time or another . These reasons are usually complicated and difficult to unravel, but often this is associated with an unsustainable bubble - for example credit debt, property prices - that drives countries towards totally unrealistic expectations.

Such happened in 2008, after half a century of economic progress, to Ireland and Iceland - two out of the nine small European countries. Like other countries, after considerable pain, they will get over their problems. The doom and gloom has been overdone.

When the United States hit its major problems - the Civil War and the Wall Street crash - there were no predictions that that great democracy was done for.

Western Europe went through two major wars in the twentieth century and emerged more prosperous than ever.

Britain in the 1970s was bailed out by the International Monetary Fund and the so-called Swiss 'gnomes of Zürich'.

Britain too faces considerable pain before it overcomes its present parlous economic situation.

Two other major arguments

The Human Development Index (HDI)

But economic welfare, while important, is not everything. The Human Development Index (HDI) does include standards of living, but also includes life expectancy, literacy and education statistics. It offers a more rounded view of a country's actual quality of life, as opposed to a simple economic performance. Again, it is remarkable how many small countries fill the top places. The latest (2010) estimates for European OECD member countries are as follows (population under 11 million in bold):

1 **Norway** 2 **Ireland** 3 Netherlands 4 **Sweden** 5 Germany 6 **Switzerland**
7 France 8 **Finland** 9 **Iceland** 10 **Belgium** 11 **Denmark** 12 Spain
13 Greece 14 Italy 15 **Luxembourg** 16 **Austria** 17 Britain
18 **Czech Republic** 19 **Slovenia** 20 **Slovakia**

And finally ... Income Inequality

Many believe that gross income inequality is a factor in the breakdown of social cohesion. In western Europe it is once again the Scandinavians that have the greatest equality of income. Here are the figures:

1 **Denmark** 2 **Sweden** 3 **Norway** 4 **Finland** 5 Germany 6 **Austria**
7 Netherlands 8 France 9 **Belgium** 10 **Switzerland** 11 **Ireland** 12 Greece
13 Spain 14 Italy 15 Britain 16 **Portugal**

Again, and dramatically, it is the small countries that lead the way.

With independence, Scotland could easily be among them.

SI 985 March 2011

CHAPTER 27

Some of the Election Arguments

Without the Union, Scotland could by now have been very wealthy indeed

Dear Reader,

You will probably receive this month's edition of the Scots Independent during the first week in April. That means that this may be the last occasion for me to give you my own summary of arguments in favour of independence and the SNP government to put to the voters before the Scottish elections on 5 May. (There will be another one before May, but the vagaries of our current postal system?)

So here goes.

Independence gives Responsibility and Dignity

Everyone accepts that is right and proper for a mature and healthy individual to stand on his own two feet. It gives you responsibility, and dignity. You become part of society, rather than a scrounging hanger-on.

So it is with individual nations.

No-one should give the time of day to folk or nations that are quite able to look after themselves, but instead deliberately refuse responsibility, and hold out their hands to scrounge off others.

Yet basically, that is what Tory, Labour and Lib Dem parties want us Scots to do: hold out the begging bowl to the English and scrounge off them. How contemptible.

Too Small - Piffle!

But, some argue, Scotland is too small and would be too poor to stand on its own: we need English subsidies to keep us at our present living standards.

This is total and complete piffle - it is the small countries of north-western Europe that are far and away the richest, fairest, best-run, most democratic and most advanced countries not just in Europe, but in the world. And that has been the case for decades.

No need for them to scrounge off anyone, and no need for Scotland either.

Without the Union, Scotland could by now have been very wealthy indeed, but instead we are among the poorest.

Britain lags further and further behind - and drags Scotland down with it.

It is a national disgrace that Britain since the late 1970s has gained billions of pounds from oil in Scottish waters - and squandered it.

The So-called Union Dividend

The so-called Union dividend is a myth. Not only has the UK Union made Scotland far poorer than it could be, it has led to mass emigration, gross disparity of wealth, and a disregard of Scotland's interests.

Typically, Labour MSP Jackie Baillie thinks that planting Britain's only nuclear weapons arsenal at Faslane is a great part of the Union dividend.

No other small democratic country would tolerate it.

As Part of Britain

As part of Britain, Scotland's wealth has been squandered on nuclear weapons, Trident submarines and illegal wars for half a century.

And as part of Britain we shall continue to host dangerous WMD at Faslane, close to our greatest centres of population.

As part of Britain, we shall continue to live in a country with just about the greatest disparities in wealth in western Europe, where the greedy richest grab all they can and leave the ordinary hard-working Scot miles behind. And Westminster governments do nothing.

And Finally ...

At this election we must make the arguments for independence. But we must also make the arguments for the SNP government.

So don't forget: the achievements of the SNP government - the most striking examples:

- Council tax frozen
- Prescription charges ended
- 1,000 more police on the street
- Crime at a 32-year low
- Accident and emergency units saved

- Forth and Tay bridge tolls ended
- Free university tuition fees
- Smaller class sizes
- 330 schools built or refurbished
- Shorter hospital waiting times
- 25,000 new apprenticeships
- Free personal care for the elderly protected
- Free bus passes kept
and many many more.

And don't forget, either: never, ever, believe a word of what you read in the papers about the SNP!

SI 986 April 2011

CHAPTER 28

Parallels and Contrasts: the US and Scotland

The American 'No' to Independence

The American Declaration of Independence was adopted in Philadelphia by the Second Continental Congress on 4 July 1776.

And yet, when, just ten years before, the British House of Commons had asked the great American Benjamin Franklin about 'the temper of the Americans towards Great Britain before the year 1763', Franklin had replied that it was 'the best in the world'.

The colonists, Franklin said, 'submitted willingly to the government of the Crown, and paid, in all their courts, obedience to acts of Parliament ... The colonists were governed by this country (Britain) at the expense only of a little pen, ink, and paper. They were led by a thread ... Natives of England were always treated with particular regard.'

You can be assured that had the Americans been asked in 1763 if they would vote for independence in the then unheard-of device of a national referendum, they would have voted with a resounding 'No'.

So why, just twelve years later, were the colonies at war with Britain, and one year later declaring their independence, did they go for independence?

The American 'Yes' to Independence

The fact is that the century between 1665 and 1765 had seen massive developments in America. Almost unnoticed by the outside world, huge structural changes had been taking place.

As historian Isaac Kramnick says:

'Long-term factors were at work which made the connection a less than perfect one.'

By 1765 local political élites had established themselves and popularly elected lower houses of assembly had been set up in each colony.

From being a small, remote and relatively unimportant colony, the American population had grown some tenfold, approaching two million, and production had greatly increased as had the amount of land settled.

America was by 1765 hugely important as a trading partner for a Britain impoverished by wars.

Kramnick again:

'Far from the colonies being weak and dependent subsidiaries of Britain, it

66

would appear that the British economy was fast dependent on the colonies. ... Fearful of the disastrous consequences to Britain of a loss of control over the colonies, the British government sought not only to maintain but to intensify its economic and political hegemony.'

It needed just a decade of incompetence, arrogance and insensitivity from London, inspired leadership in America and a new belief in independence among the people to set America free.

Sound familiar?

The Scottish Parallel

At long last, Scotland now has its own popularly elected national body in the Holyrood Parliament. (Although most members still offer docile support for the policies of their London masters.)

Scotland, too, was always important to the British Empire - as a source of soldiers and sailors, well-educated administrators and engineers, and workers to produce ships, locomotives and much else.

More recently, Scotland has been as a useful possession far from London for weapons of mass destruction and weapons testing.

And Scotland now, like America in the 18th century, is incredibly important to London as a source of great wealth - oil wealth this time.

Following years of political incompetence, by the mid-1970s Britain ended up as an economic basket case, and future taxes from Scottish oil wealth were the promised collateral for the immense bail-outs from the IMF, Switzerland and Germany.

In the following years our oil wealth was squandered, frittered away, then wasted on wars. It has even been claimed by cynical unionist politicians that the oil wealth has really all gone. Sadly, all too many believed them.

Now we know that, as Britain's economic problems have returned with a vengeance, a great part of the solution is - Scotland's oil wealth - once again.

Of course, there are differences. America did not suffer from the intense centralisation, indeed globalisation, that has been Scotland's lot for the last fifty plus years.

But taken in the round the American experience of the road to independence can be an inspiration to Scots as we move forward to take our own place in the world of nations.

SI 987 May 2011

CHAPTER 29

The night the earth moved.

Some reflections on and after a momentous Scottish Election Night

The Conservatives have struggled for years to get back as serious players in Scottish politics. There are no signs that they can make much progress in the next decade.

The Liberal Democrats are now in a far worse position even than the Tories, and it could take them thirty years to make a come-back, if they ever manage it.

And if Labour prove as inept over the next five years as they have done over the last four, their share of the vote could easily fall another 5% to 8%.

Anyone for a bet on an even greater SNP majority in 2015?

And as the Alternative Vote fell victim to negativity, what does that tell us?

Under our roughly proportional system, the final election result was as follows:

SNP 69 (53.5%) Labour 37 (28.7%) Tory 15 (11.6%) LD 5 (3.9%) Green 2 (1.6%) IND 1 (0.8%)

The first-past-the-post element (used for 73 seats) resulted in the following:

SNP 53 (72.6%) Labour 15 (20.5%) Tory 3 (4.1%) LD 2 (2.7%) Others 0 (1.1%)

Under first-past-the-post, David Cameron's 'fair, simple tried-and-tested system that has served us well' the result would have been as follows (out of Holyrood's 129 seats):

SNP 94 (72.8%) Labour 27 (20.9%) Tory 5 (3.9%) LD 4 (2.3%) Others 0

Makes you think, eh?

And there were fifteen favourite reasons we won :

1 A huge psychological breakthrough in 2007, so we Scots knew that Labour could be beaten.
2 A very competent SNP government doing its best to improve life in Scotland.
3 An appalling, negative and hypocritical opposition stopping necessary reforms.
4 An excellent 'Question Time' performance by Alex Salmond that floored the opposition.
5 A brilliant up-beat campaign with fun, humour and a positive outlook.

6 A desperate flight from heckler to sandwich-bar

7 A brilliant SNP television broadcast that showed viewers our achievements.

8 A negative ill-judged Labour campaign with policies stolen from the SNP.

9 A rotten Labour TV broadcast that highlighted a moaning - supposedly Labour - family.

10 An important leaflet campaign to show voters why the second vote is so vital.

11 'Re-elect': a wonderful word to be able to use.

12 A negative Unionist press campaign that was so at odds with the facts it was risible.

13 A despised Westminster coalition

14 Positive voters who refused to be cowed by negative unionism or a ludicrous press.

15 A positive record, team, vision message versus a negative, backwards-looking whine.

And then we had the Three Graces of Lanarkshire!

Rutherglen, fourth safest Labour seat, was the first result, and early, at 12.45. Labour held it, but the swing was about 9%, said the pundits, and the Liberals lost their deposit.

Next up at 1.15 was East Kilbride. Linda Fabiani was the candidate, elegant and composed, and as she stood on the stage in the moments before the announcement I scrutinised her face for any sign to give the result away. Nothing. I thought, 'We've lost.'

The votes were announced. It took time to sink in that Linda had won the first sensational SNP victory of election night, with a 6.5% majority.

And what a marvellous speech she made, happy, generous, and stretching out a sympathetic hand to her defeated opponents, especially Labour's Andy Kerr, the previous incumbent.

Mr Kerr made an amusing, self deprecating reply, which did him a lot of good. Sadly it was undone in an interview shortly after, when he declared that from tomorrow he was out to 'undermine' Linda. Well, well - lost it.

Fifteen minutes later it was Hamilton's turn. Hamilton! Iconic seat - I hope Winnie was watching.

Christina McKelvie - another 'Flag in the Wind' contributor - was our stunning candidate here and won a stunning victory over Labour's Tom McCabe . Like Linda, she made a first-rate speech of acceptance, this time perhaps with a hint of emotion in her voice. Not surprising, after so many years Hamilton was back with the SNP. This time the majority was 8.7%

This wonderful evening for Lanarkshire was completed forty minutes later when the results for Clydesdale came in. Clydesdale meant a lot to me personally as I had worked there in the late 1970s for the late Tom MacAlpine. We just missed it in October 1974.

But candidate Aileen Campbell - youngest MSP in the 2007 intake - came romping home with a great victory over Labour's Karen Gillon. Again, she looked elegant and spoke so well. This time, the majority soared to 14.1%.

So thank you, Linda, Christina and Aileen. Your elegance, intelligence, decency and grace did the party proud that night.

As election nights go, it doesn't get much better than that.

SI 988 June 2011

Now, the next step..

CHAPTER 30

Winning the Referendum (1)

The SNP must give its members the vital facts.

Winning the Independence Referendum will not be easy.

We can expect a united opposition in the press that will stoop to all kinds of smears, lies and innuendos to undermine the independence movement. What can we do about it?

The great thing about the election on 5 May was that the SNP government had a record of achievement. In spite of everything the press threw at us, the voters at large were not taken in by the scare stories.

Unfortunately, for the referendum, we cannot point to an established record of an independent Scotland.

Key Facts from Small Countries

But fortunately, what we do have, however, is the excellent established records of other small (under 11 million people) independent countries in northern Europe.

Of these nine countries, seven are recognised as among the most advanced in the world, be it by the overall human development index, health and education, life expectancy, low infant mortality, freedom from corruption, fairness of income distribution or living standards by Gross Domestic Product. (I'll try to come back to these with more details in future articles.)

So we must arm ourselves with all the facts we can, showing just how successful these small countries have been. It is vital that the SNP provides its members with the vital facts, so that we can show how incredibly successful these small countries are in giving their peoples the highest standards of living in the world.

Educating the Public about Scotland

Time and time again I hear Scots who have been brainwashed by politicians and the media lamenting the state of Scotland. Many of the complaints can be summed up in the sentence: 'There's nothing left up here.'

Well, of course, the great heavy industries have gone. The great days of shipbuilding on the Clyde and the great locomotive works in Springburn, Glasgow, have disappeared. The old coal fields have closed. Steelworks have gone from Motherwell and Wishaw.

With the end of Empire and new technologies some of this was inevitable.

But many changes for the worse could have been avoided. Control of our newspapers and media has largely passed outside, as has the control of our great publishing houses (e.g. Nelson, Collins, Blackie).

But in spite of all this, Scotland is very far from being a wasteland.

Clearly, for our five million population we still have a great deal of fertile land to raise cattle and sheep, to grow cereals and fruit, we still have great seas and coastlines for fishing and fish-farming.

And the land and seas themselves attract tourists for all kinds of recreation: walking climbing, biking, diving, even surfing.

Our universities and language schools attract thousands of students from all over the world.

Roads, bridges, houses and premises of all kinds need building and maintenance. Transport alone needs tens of thousands of employees.

We need employees to work in shops from small specialist outlets to supermarkets, from Apple Mac stores to fish and chip shops.

We need joiners, plumbers, electricians, gardeners and many more.

There are literally millions involved in all kinds of economic activity, as there are in every small country in Europe.

What we really need is a competent government of our own, responsive to the changes that are required.

More to Come!

Next month I would like to deal with two other aspects of winning the referendum.

Firstly, we must counter the assertion - and it is no more than that - that 'the Union has served us well'.

In fact, the very opposite is the case, and we must say so bluntly, with facts and figures to back our arguments up.

Secondly, we must learn how to deal with certain questions that are always being posed by Unionists. And once again, no prisoners should be taken!

SI 989 July 2011

CHAPTER 31

Winning the Referendum (2)

Unionists have relied on negativity

In July's edition of the Scots Independent I said that this month I would write about, firstly, the Unionist assertion the 'the Union has served us well' and secondly how we should deal with certain questions posed by those opposed to independence. But that will have to wait.

Out of the blue I noticed an article in The Scotsman of Wednesday 20 July by one Sam Ghibaldan, who it transpires was a special adviser to LibDem deputy first minister Jim Wallace. Its title was 'Salmond's opponents must get the ball rolling' followed by a sub-heading 'A "no to independence" campaign must stress not just what the UK does for Scotland, but what Scotland does for the UK'.

Great, I thought. Just up my street. Play it again Sam and let's have all your arguments laid out for examination.

Alas, it was not to be. Two thirds of the article were spent considering the Unionist referendum organisation against independence; bemoaning the fact that the SNP had a head start in the campaign, and that 'political heavyweights capable of taking on Salmond in debate are ... in short supply.'

To be fair, he does go on to admit that 'opponents of independence haven't needed to give a great deal of thought to the case for remaining part of the UK.' (We've known that for a long time.) They have relied on the 'negative narrative' that 'Scotland would be a lot poorer if it were independent.'

So let's take that one first. On the contrary, Scotland independent would be much wealthier than at present.

Opponents of independence should be asked just why, exactly, Scotland would be poorer, when the history of small nations in northern Europe proves exactly the opposite.

Those that have succeeded in remaining independent or winning their independence from aggressive dominating neighbours do far better than Scotland.

And because of Norway's own oil (found in the 1960s, just like Scotland's), which she has managed for the benefit of her own people, Norway has emerged as one of the most prosperous countries in the world, leaving Scotland far behind.

So the Unionist assertion that Scotland independent would be poorer should be constantly challenged, for it is nonsense.

Sam claims that his assertion is backed up as 'the UK taxpayers bailed out the Scottish banks.'

Wrong again, Sam. For a straightforward answer to that see Joan McAlpine: Scotland and the banking bailout - time for the truth - Go Lassie Go at **http://joanmcalpine.typepad.com/joan_mcalpine/2011/07/scotland-and-the-banking-bailout-time-for-the-truth.html**

And scroll down to the bottom to read the actual transcript of the conversation between Derek Bateman and Professors Walker and Campbell. (George Walker, Professor of International Finance Law at Queen Mary University, London and also Glasgow University, and Andrew Campbell, Professor of International and Finance Law at Leeds University)

The one other reason he advances for the Union is 'the close-knit family, business and cultural relationships within the British Isles'.

It's a rather sentimental reason to allow British governments we never voted for to steal and squander our resources and keep us with lower standards than any other country in northern Europe.

Finally, having admitted that in the past the Unionists have relied on scare stories that Scotland would be 'a lot poorer if it were independent ' - scare stories designed to undermine the confidence of Scots and keep them in the UK - and that this approach has 'considerable resonance', astonishingly, Mr Ghibaldan then claims that 'being part of the UK is a clear expression of the confidence of Scots both in Scotland and their ability to be an effective part of a larger, national geographical entity.'

Incredible! Try and undermine Scottish confidence about independence to keep them in the Union, and then claim that by staying with the Union the Scots are showing their confidence!

So Mr Ghibaldan's article is short on reasons for the Union and ends with a gross hypocrisy.

It's as convincing in its logic as David Cameron's 'I don't believe in Scottish independence' or Nick Clegg's belief that being independent 'is an extremely risky thing to do'.

Don't believe a word these chancers tell you!

SI 990 August 2011

CHAPTER 32

Winning the referendum (3)

Scotland lags behind other small nations.

In a letter published in the Herald newspaper on 8 August, a Mr Ronnie Martin concludes as follows: *'Scotland and England have been good for each other for 300 years and they will be good for each other for another 300 years.'*

Can this possibly be true?

Just think about it for a moment. For over 300 years (or 400, if you take the Union of the Crowns in 1603 as your starting point) Scotland has benefited from this Union?

Day by day, week by week, month by month, year by year for at least 300 years we have been the beneficiaries of this Union, surely the best of all possible political systems.

No other nation on earth has been so lucky. Surely we must then be the most fortunate, the most contented, the wealthiest, and the happiest of peoples.

And surely other nations must be lining up to join our Union, anxious to dissolve their own parliaments and rush their peoples' representatives into the bosom of Westminster, the best, the most decent, the most incorruptible of all such institutions.

OK, the French are too big and proud to want to join (although England did try very hard to extend London rule there as well, until Joan of Arc put a stop to that nonsense).

And the Germans seem to have a strange federal system which most agree works pretty well.

But what about those other, smaller, states? What about little Norway, Denmark, Finland and Switzerland? What about Sweden?

None of these benighted nations have had the benefit of the Union. For three hundred years they have had to manage without the blessings the Union has showered on Scotland.

Some - like Denmark, Sweden and Switzerland - have for centuries actually stood on their own two feet and been responsible for running their own affairs.

Some - like Norway and Finland - have even been minor parts of other Unions and have had the temerity to break away and become independent.

Surely they must envy all the benefits that Scotland enjoys from the Union - punching above our weight in the world, acting as poodles to presidents of the United States, invading foreign countries and starting illegal wars, and seldom getting a government we actually voted for.

The Union with England has given us all these things. And could it not do the same for other small European countries?

Surely they are all too small and weak to exist in the modern world?

And yet, with singular obtuseness, they do not wish to join us.

Why can this be?

Well, it seems these small independent European states really enjoy being among the most advanced, democracies in the world.

They are also amongst the wealthiest and most stable.

In 2010 they were all comfortably ahead of Britain in GDP per head.

In the same year they were also all in considerable surplus on their balance of payments.

Out of 191 countries, Norway and Switzerland were in 5th and 7th positions. Sweden, Denmark and Finland in 16th, 21st and 33rd positions.

Britain was in massive balance of payments deficit and in 186th place out of the 191.

In almost every measured area concerning human welfare, they have left Britain far behind, be it doctors per head of population, teachers per head of school populations, perception of corruption (no surprise there!), levels of crime, and income distribution, among others.

So, all things considered, it seems that the 'boasted advantages' of the Union wither away when they are compared with the advantages of independence.

And finally - for the point needs to be rammed home, time and again, in every way possible - here are some basic questions for our Unionist friends.

If Scotland has been part of this Union which for three centuries has been doing us so much good, why is it that these other small countries which have not had such benefits and are independent are so far ahead of us in almost every way?

Why is it that most recent figures show that Scotland has to share a British balance of payments **deficit** of over 40 billion dollars, while Norway has a **surplus** of over 60 billion dollars?

The fact is the Union is a disaster for Scotland and the sooner we vote to leave, the better.

SI 991 September 2011

CHAPTER 33

Winning the Referendum (4)

Countering silly spins and daft questions

One of the clearest lessons that the May elections held for any politician was that in the end voters are scunnered by constant negativity.

I am amazed that the Labour party still has not learned that lesson.

As a former Liberal, I am even more amazed that the Liberal Democrats are following the same daft line, aided and abetted by their Coalition partners (who are wisely keeping in the background).

Jo Grimond, the intelligent, decent man who first sparked my interest in politics, must be turning in his grave at the charlatans who now purport to speak for the Liberal party.

First up is Michael Moore, MP. The same Mr Moore who thought before the election that the position of Scottish Secretary should be abolished - that is, until he himself was offered the job. Then it was all change.

Coalition Spin v SNP Promises

Last May, the SNP decisively won the Scottish election on Alex Salmond's promise to seek more powers for the Scottish parliament in the meantime and to hold a referendum on independence in the second half of the Parliament's term.

Now Mr Moore criticises Mr Salmond for 'obsessing' about these issues.

Fancy being charged with 'obsessing' about promises you made to the electorate!

Mind you, the way the LibDems have abandoned their own promises to the voters, maybe they do find the idea of keeping your promises a quaint aberration to their dishonest norm.

Next Mr Moore makes a feeble attempt to compare the legitimacy of the Westminster government's rule in Scotland to the SNP's outright victory five months ago.

He claims 'Scotland has two governments - distinct, elected and legitimate'. Well, they are certainly distinct. And they are both elected: the Westminster government by the voters of England, and the Holyrood government by the voters of Scotland.

In fact, in terms of the popular vote the London parties that now rule over us in Scotland came third and fourth in 2010. Certainly not elected by the Scots. And legitimate, Mr Moore? Hardly.

The third criticism of Mr Salmond is that he is asking for extra powers on Corporation Tax, alcohol tax, Crown Estate revenue, broadcasting and representation in Europe.

And why not, if your taxes from our own land and products are first purloined and then squandered by London? And if our so-called Scottish 'national' broadcasting service is controlled from London and a shadow of what it should be? And if our representation in Europe is half that of other nations of the same size?

Of course these are wrongs that need righting.

It's not surprising that one correspondent to the Herald advised Mr Moore to stop

'behaving like a colonial governor telling the leader of the natives what he can and can't do'.

Look Carefully at these Questions

Having attempted to establish his dubious credentials as Scottish Secretary (he's really only there because of the corrupt voting system and the fact that the Tories wouldn't dare risk taking the position for their sole Scottish MP), Mr Moore goes on to pose six questions to Mr Salmond.

Now here's a thing about political questions. Be on your guard. The first thing to ask yourself is this: Is the questioner asking in good faith or bad? Is the questioner genuinely seeking an answer, or is he simply trying to score political points?

Could the questioner ask his own party the same question and expect a reasonable answer? Indeed, is there a reasonable answer to the question?

Does the question ask for details? And do these details relate to the future?

Only if you can satisfy yourself about these points should the questioner be treated seriously.

Next month I shall try to analyse in detail the questions Mr Moore has asked of Mr Salmond and you can judge whether or not Mr Moore is sincere or insincere, whether he asks the questions in good faith or in bad faith, whether or not he is seeking answers or scoring points.

In short, is he a trustworthy person at all?

SI 992 October 2011

CHAPTER 34

Winning the referendum (5)

Tory sycophant Michael Moore's six "big" questions.

In last month's edition of the Scot Independent I said I would return to the six so-called 'big questions' put by Liberal Democrat Scotland Secretary Michael Moore, MP.

Here they are.

Question 1: What regulation would be applied to Scotland's banks and financial services and who would enforce it?

Question 2: Which currency would Scotland adopt and how could entry and influence be guaranteed?

Question 3: How would membership of international organisations, including the EU, be assured?

Question 4: What would be Scotland's defence posture be and how would its armed forces be configured?

Question 5: How many billions of pounds would Scots inherit in pension liabilities and who would pay for future pensions?

Question 6: How much would independence cost?

Doing London's Dirty Work

Mr Moore has of course been sent up by the high heid yins in London to try and spike the Scottish government. The Tories are so unpopular in Scotland that they need a fall guy to do their dirty work.

You would think that as Scottish Secretary Mr Moore would consider it his duty to work with the Scottish government and put the wishes of the Scottish people to the British cabinet. But that's not how British politics works. His real paymasters are down south.

Now of course when you look at Mr Moore's six questions carefully a pattern begins to emerge.

They are all about the future (five to ten years down the line), which no-one, not even Mr Moore, can forecast with any certainty. He should know, for

79

many of the promises he and his party made before the general election in 2010, in May, were broken by June.

Mr Moore's questions also ask for detail about the future, which again no-one can forecast. Again, Mr Moore knows this only too well.

In fact, Mr Moore's questions are not serious questions at all. None of them are asked in good faith. None of them can seriously expect an exact answer.

They all seek to give the impression that independence for Scotland would be incredibly difficult to achieve and fraught with danger. That is their main purpose.

So why ask these Questions now?

Let's put the questions into context. Never before has the Scottish National Party with its policy of independence been so successful. Never before has our party - or any party - gained an outright majority in the Scottish parliament. Never before have we offered such a threat to the status quo and to those who uphold it.

So Westminster politicians are afraid, especially Scottish Westminster politicians. And it is plain fear that is behind all of Mr Moore's questions.

They are deliberately, insincerely and cynically posed to instil doubt into the Scottish people about independence. It really is Douglas Alexander's old agenda: the engendering of fear.

These questions are designed to trap the naive and to discredit the SNP, the Scottish people and the very idea of national independence - an idea that is accepted by all but the most backward-looking and arrogant of states.

'The Day of Questions'

Although I am not a religious person, as I read Mr Moore's questions I was reminded of a famous chapter in the Bible: Luke 20.

This chapter describes what is sometimes called 'The Day of Questions', when the increasingly uneasy Jewish high heid yins get their people to try to trap and discredit Jesus by asking what they think is a clever and difficult question.

They are soundly defeated.

They try a second time. But they are by now so afraid of the people that they send others in their place, who pretend to be sincere. But Jesus 'sees through their subtle deception'.

So again they are confounded.

They give up, but along come another lot, the Sadducees, a group that is 'few but very wealthy'. (Sounds like David Cameron's cabinet.) They are also, according to one great scholar, 'largely collaborationist with Rome, being unwilling to risk losing their wealth, their comfort and their place'. (All these parallels!)

They ask a third question, but once more the questioners are routed.

Insincere Questions are no good

So insincere questions asked in bad faith are in the end worthless. Indeed, they are counter-productive. They leave a bad taste in the mouth and people in the end see through them. It is the questioner who ends up confounded.

My own Questions for Mr Moore

For each of his questions, if Mr Moore would care to replace the word 'Scotland' with the phrase 'the rump of the UK' and give us detailed answers which will apply between five and ten years down the line, then we may be able to have a dialogue.

But I doubt if he will be able to.

Such are the failures of Britain's regulatory services, such has been the decline in the pound over the years, such is the stupidity of question 3, such is the chaos of Britain's ever-changing friends and enemies and of its armed forces procurement, such is Britain's massive debt, goodness knows how the poor soul would be able to answer.

As for how much independence would cost: just ask the Norwegians, Mr Moore, just ask the Norwegians!

SI 993 November 2011

CHAPTER 35

Winning the referendum (6)

The Need for Courtesy, Decency and Moderation

The Scottish National Party is particularly fortunate in the attitude of its leadership when faced with attacks, sneers and condescension from opponents on television and radio programmes. This can come from political opponents, but equally from presenters such as David Dimbleby, Jeremy Paxman, Jo Cockburn, Kirsty Wark (all TV) and Gary Robertson (Radio Scotland).

Alex Salmond, Nicola Sturgeon, and John Swinney, in particular, are especially good at staying unruffled in the face of attack, and biding their time, without interruption.

I well remember a Question Time programme last spring when Alex spoke for a total of less than seven minutes. But when he did speak it was devastating. Unlike other politicians, who often treat the programme as a party political broadcast, an exercise in patronising and/or point scoring, Alex Salmond set out to teach the audience about the Lockerbie tragedy and the dangers faced by the English and Welsh health service.

The rapt expressions on the faces of the listeners said it all.

SNP party members in general should always be courteous to our opponents. (And never forget that how we deal with our most determined opponents is often being watched by other uncommitted voters.) Some opponents, such as Labour's Ian Davidson, scarcely deserve it, but many others have succumbed to three centuries of unionist propaganda. They genuinely believe that the Union is great and Scotland too small to be independent.

As the great Tom Paine said in his introduction to 'Common Sense':

'A long habit of not thinking a thing wrong, gives it a superficial of being right.'

'Time makes more converts than reason.'

It takes time, but they can be won over. They will not be won over by ranting, overbearing personalities.

What goes for the leadership and party members in general goes equally for student leaders, be they ever so high, or councillors, MSPs, MPs and MEPs, be they ever so low.

I recently saw some exchanges in a local paper between an SNP councillor and his Labour opponent. It made for depressing reading. They were both determined to have the last word, and the whole thing left a bit of a nasty taste in the mouth. It did neither of them any good.

Finally, on this point, we all have our own little obsessions. We find it hard to believe that people can disagree with us without being bigots. It is all the harder to take when it is someone in our own party. But that does not excuse intemperate language in any debate. The public at large is fed up with quarrelling politicians. If they are members of the same party it can only do that party damage, sometimes serious.

Using the Negative

I have always been a great believer in positive campaigning. Last May the SNP's positive attitude was almost certainly **the** major difference between us and the other parties and it paid off, in spades.

But there can also be a place for a negative message.

Think back to the Alternative Vote (AV) referendum last May. OK, there wasn't much happening in Scotland.

But down south, the anti-AV campaign was quite incredibly negative, emphasising any arguments they could dream up to put the fear of death into the electorate. They also told many lies about the AV system. (Negativity and lies - remind you of anything? They're already doing the same here, three or four years before the independence referendum.)

The pro-AV campaign tried to explain the advantages of the Alternative Vote, but they were overwhelmed by the ferocity of their opponents' onslaught.

Not only that, but the pro campaign totally failed to highlight the preposterous results - and the dire consequences - of the first-past-the-post system.

The result was that over a period between May 2010 and May 2011 - the AV side went from a commanding lead in the polls - 59% to 32% - to a devastating loss - 32% to 68%.

There were other factors involved, of course, but the appalling campaign run by the First Past The Post protagonists played an emphatic part.

Let us learn from this. We must not resort to lies, which would only come back and haunt us.

But we should not hesitate to use the incredible number of arguments which highlight the severe disadvantage of belonging to the United Kingdom.

We should particularly emphasise those arguments that people already agree with. Here are just a few. (It might be useful if the Scots Independent would think of publishing a couple of articles along these lines.)

Everybody knows that Britain once ruled a great empire. Those days are well and truly over.

But still British politicians act as if we were a major world power. We spend incredible amounts on defence, sometimes twice that of other European countries. We just can't afford it.

Here in Scotland, more often than not we get a government that we never voted for. For Scotland, our political system is simply undemocratic and illegitimate.

And our own country's wealth, which could yet help turn us into a wealthy north European country, has been squandered and frittered by arrogant and incompetent politicians at Westminster.

SI 994 December 2011

Ian Roy Goldie
8th February 1941 – 2nd December 2011

I had known Ian since some time in the Seventies, as I had met him at an SNP meeting in Lanark, but only had occasional, always very amicable, contacts with him over the years.

Ian's involvement with the Scots Independent started in January 2004, when I shanghaied him into becoming one of the compilers of the SI's internet issue, The Flag in the Wind; he continued in this role right up to his death. When I became the SI Editor in November 2005, I poached him for that too. Ian's first column was in January 2006, and he eventually inherited the coveted back page, which he retained also right up to the end. It was very fitting that his last column had the sub heading "The need for courtesy, decency and moderation", as these had been his watchwords all the time I knew him. He was completely dependable, and always worth reading; the one word which could describe Ian was "Positive". He abhorred negativity, although he recognised it was sometimes necessary, but did not regard it as desirable. His place in the SI will be difficult to fill.

Ian was born in Glasgow, and educated in Glasgow, Hamilton and Islay; his secondary education was at Hutchesons', Glasgow, and he excelled at rugby, being described as a very quick wing three quarter. As far as can be gathered he was pretty good at tennis as well.

He graduated from Glasgow University, with an Honours Degree in modern language (French and German) and a Certificate in Industrial Administration; he also had periods of study at the Universities of Paris and Tubingen.

After working in marketing and advertising in London, he returned to Scotland in 1967, did a teacher's training course at Jordanhill and became a teacher of modern languages; at the time of his retiral in 1995 he was principal teacher of modern languages at Lanark Grammar School.

He joined the SNP in 1967, and was a local government candidate once, a Westminster parliamentary candidate four times, and a European candidate twice. In 2005 he used his talents as Election Agent for Colin Beattie, in Midlothian, where he helped increase the vote by 25%.

He was a very active member of the SNP, and was at the Referendum Road Show, and a Branch meeting the week he died. Like all of us in the SNP he was absolutely delighted and overwhelmed at the SNP success in the Scottish Election.

Ian was very much a family man, and in 2011, a family group of 21 went on a week's holiday to Islay, where they had many happy memories; his father had been Chief Customs Officer at the Laphroig Distillery there! They stayed at a farmhouse close by the ruins of the stronghold of the Lords of the Isles.

It was interesting to hear that he met his wife Margaret on a David Urquhart bus tour to the Isle of Wight; I do not know if he knew David Urquhart, but he also is another SNP member of the same vintage as ourselves.

Ian left a sister, Joyce, a son, John, and daughter, Claire, (married to a Norwegian and a Spaniard respectively) and two step-daughters; he and his wife Margaret, had eleven grandchildren – Sean, Ross, Christoffer, Kerry, Murray, Sophia, Steffen, James, Alex, Sara and Aidan. He was a loving and much loved grand father to them all, and will be sorely missed.

Jim Lynch, with assistance from Joyce McIver, Gordon Hepburn and Colin Beattie MSP.

Ian on the extended family holiday to Islay in 2011

Scottish Gold

i.m. Ian Goldie 1941- 2011

Some men are base metal,
dull and leaden,
they spread misery and weigh us down
with dark intentions
and dark deeds.

Some men are alloys.
superficially bright,
lighting life up for a while,
before they tarnish, become lacklustre,
and the base metal shows black
through the tinsel.

Some men are gold,
golden to the very core;
24 carat gold
that never discolours,
its brightness never dimming.

We had a friend who was pure gold;
good and true in the essence of his being,
he held his convictions without malice,
he debated without rancour,
he inspired us, and made us glad
to be his comrades in arms.

He left us suddenly,
but his voice is with us still,
resounding like music in the inner ear
and his smile gleams in the memory
like fine gold,
Scottish gold.

David C Purdie

List of Subscribers – as at 20th July 2012.

Denholm & Myra Christie, Kincardine on Forth.

Bill & Catriona Clark, Banknock, Falkirk .

Margaret and Jim Cuthbert, Edinburgh

Kenneth Fraser, St Andrews

Margaret Goldie, Edinburgh

Ian Hudghton, Forfar

John Hunter-Paterson, Dundonald, Kilmarnock

Alastair Kidd, Edinburgh

Jim Lynch, Edinburgh

Graeme McAllan, Orlando, Florida.

Keith McCartney, St Andrews

Bruce McIver, St Andrews

Iain McIver, St Andrews

Joyce McIver, St Andrews

Paul McIver, St Andrews

Scott McIver, St Andrews

Donald Macleod, Bridge of Don, Aberdeen

Joan McNair, Glasgow

Hamish MacQueen, Glasgow

Iain Ramsay, Greenock

Paul Henderson Scott, Edinburgh

David Urquhart, East Kilbride